## Methuen Playscripts

The Methuen Playscripts series exists to extend the range of plays in print by publishing work which is not yet widely known but which has already earned a place in the acting repertoire of the modern theatre.

## Man Friday & Mind Your Head

Originally performed as a TV play on BBC1's *Play for Today* in 1972, *Man Friday* was later adapted for the stage and toured by John McGrath's 7:84 Company and the Nottingham Playhouse Theatre in Education Company. A lively satire on British imperialism, it tells the story of Robinson Crusoe, an English Puritan tormented by conscience, as seen through the eyes of Man Friday.

'Bracing theatrical fun and musical inventiveness . . . extremely beguiling . . . I feel that if there is any hope for popular musical theatre in Britain it lies in this direction rather than in an attempt to do pastiche Broadway.'
Michael Billington, The *Guardian*

*Mind Your Head* was commissioned and staged by the Liverpool Everyman Theatre in 1973 and later performed by the Dolphin Company at the Shaw Theatre, London in 1974.

'A wonderful show is *Mind Your Head* . . . It's great, rowdy, accessible popular theatre. It combines a jokey reworking of the Hamlet myth with a bus journey from Hampstead to Pimlico on a distinctly twisted bus. It's bumptiously on the right side politically, is full of extraordinary characters, and is not afraid to switch the mood from gaiety to bitter seriousness. The script is clearly the work of a poet who's come to grips with the way imaginative expression can be made to work in popular forms . . . '
*Time Out Magazine*

*by the same author*

*Poetry*
POEMS (Cape)
OUT LOUD (Cape Goliard)
RIDE THE NIGHTMARE (Cape)
PENGUIN MODERN POETS NO 22

*Plays*
TYGER (Cape)
TAMBURLANE THE MAD HEN (*in* 'Playspace': Methuen)
Adaptation of the MARAT/SADE (Calder and Boyars)

*Novels*
IF YOU SEE ME COMIN' (Cape)
THE BODYGUARD (Cape)
WARTIME (Cape)

# MAN FRIDAY

**a play**

**music by Mike Westbrook**

# MIND YOUR HEAD

**a return trip with songs**

**music by Andy Roberts**

# ADRIAN MITCHELL

First published in Great Britain 1974
by Eyre Methuen Ltd
11 New Fetter Lane, London EC4P 4EE
Copyright © 1974 Adrian Mitchell
Music for *Man Friday*
© 1974 Mike Westbrook
Music for *Mind Your Head*
© 1974 Andy Roberts

Set by Expression Typesetters
Printed in Great Britain by
Fletcher & Son Ltd, Norwich

ISBN 0 413 31810 9 (Hardback)
ISBN 0 413 31820 6 (Paperback)

# Contents

# MAN FRIDAY

## Introduction

*Man Friday* started life as a TV play commissioned by BBC 1's Play for Today. It was directed by James MacTaggart. Colin Blakely played Crusoe and Ram John Holder was Man Friday. Half-way through writing it, I realised it could work on stage if the audience could be persuaded to represent the tribe. John McGrath's 7:84 Company toured the stage version with Roger Sloman as Crusoe and Chris Asanti as Friday. It has also been toured by the Nottingham Playhouse Theatre in Education Company.

The story is told by Man Friday to his tribe and at the end the audience is called on to make a decision about Crusoe. Crusoe is *not* a Fascist — he is a liberal. That is why the greatest violence he employs against Friday is chaining and gagging — an image which should recall Bobby Seale. His slaughter of Friday's friends is done out of ignorance and also out of his upbringing. It is nonetheless slaughter, and the audience shouldn't be allowed to forget it. Friday, we assume, comes from a well-run, cooperative tribe — there are good tribes and bad tribes of course. Friday should make his points out of innocence rather than knowing needling.

*Man Friday* was first presented on BBC1's *Play for Today* on October 30th 1972 with the following cast:

| | |
|---|---|
| FRIDAY | Ram John Holder |
| CRUSOE | Colin Blakely |
| MEMBERS OF FRIDAY'S TRIBE | George Browne |
| | Tommy Eytle |
| | Sue Chaloner |
| | Robert Atiko |
| | Gladys Taylor |

Produced by Graeme McDonald
Directed by James MacTaggart

The play was also toured by the 7:84 Theatre Company between April and June 1973 in schools, colleges, universities and community centres in the following towns: Skegness, Scunthorpe, Lincoln, Lancaster, Rochdale, Leeds, Newcastle, Manchester, Blackburn, Bingley, Bristol, Plymouth, Cambridge, York and London. The cast was as follows:

| | |
|---|---|
| FRIDAY | Christopher Asanti |
| CRUSOE | Roger Sloman |
| MEMBERS OF FRIDAY'S TRIBE | Di Rowan |
| | Vari Sylvester |
| | Paul Kessel |

Music by Mike Westbrook and performed by the Solid Gold Cadillac
Directed by Gavin Richards

Seats, either chairs or cushions, are in a semi-circle or three sides of a square.

Set, at back of acting area, consists of a section of a stockade and one corner of CRUSOE's house, which is cluttered with non-realistic props. This is a set made by the tribe to represent CRUSOE's house, not CRUSOE's actual house. So a frying pan may just be the shape of a frying pan cut out of a banana tree leaf (painted cardboard). A gun may be a threatening stick.

The TRIBE, including FRIDAY, wear jeans, bare feet, and lengths of lightweight flame-orange material draped over their shoulders. The DOCTOR may wear a fantastic head-dress designed to frighten evil spirits.

CRUSOE wears the traditional goatskin breeks, long hair, goatskin jacket and goatskin sunshade.

As the audience come in, they are greeted by the members of the TRIBE, talked with as they are shown to their seats and talked with some more while they are sitting. If possible the string player should be playing during this period, as it will take time and there'll always be someone who's not being talked with.

The TRIBE will use their own words and act in a friendly way. Items of information for the TRIBE to convey.
1. We are members of a tribe.
2. It's a small tribe and also not typical. The tribe works very well, occasional fights but nothing serious.
3. Will you join the tribe just for an hour and a half? We're going to listen to a story. Those two men (Friday and Crusoe) are going to tell the story. Friday is the tribe's Storyteller.
4. You could help the story by:
   (a) wearing or if you prefer, holding over your shoulder one of these cloaks.
   (b) playing one of a selection of cheap musical instruments during the songs.
   (c) humming during songs.
   (d) joining in discussions of the story whenever the story stops.
5. The story is important because at the end of it the tribe will decide whether Crusoe, who has asked to join the tribe, will be admitted, or whether he will be sent back to his own island.

One of the TRIBE will have to act as musical director of the audience, rehearsing them in their accompaniments before the story starts.

CRUSOE doesn't play a part in this general introduction. He lurks, somewhat anxiously, but is allowed to go up to individuals when he thinks the TRIBE are not looking and canvass in whispers for his admission to the tribe.

Towards the end of the introduction the members of the TRIBE pass among the audience with bowls of wine and lemonade, wine for adults, lemonade for kids. But FRIDAY and CRUSOE stand apart from this and are the last ones to sip the wine. They are becoming nervous because the story is important to both of them.

The other three members of the TRIBE seat themselves at the front of the audience and in turn stretch out their hands, palms upwards, towards FRIDAY. CRUSOE goes behind the set.

DOCTOR (to FRIDAY): Whether it hurts you, or whether it pleases you, whether it hurts us, or whether it pleases us. It is time for you to tell the story.

FRIDAY: It is time.

(FRIDAY takes a small drum and begins to play and move in a slow, thinking dance. YOUNG MAN begins to play his stringed instrument. All TRIBE join in accompaniment.)

(Sings.)
As we have always been together,
Let us drink together.
As we are together now,
Let us dream together.
Let the wine flow,
Let my words flow
And I will try to tell my story truly,
As truly as I worship you,
My own people.

I am going to tell you about
A redfaced monster with a man inside its belly.
I am going to tell you about
A gabbling goat who could spit deadly thunder.
I am going to tell you about
The man who walks outside,

(CRUSOE is seen pacing behind set.)

About the man who waits outside.

Close your eyes and see the story,
Close your eyes and see the story.

(FRIDAY sees that the TRIBE have closed their eyes. He closes his eyes. Storm music from the TRIBE.)

There were four of us. The night storm caught us. It broke the back of our canoe. It swallowed us all down. And then it sicked us up on to a beach we'd never seen before.

YOUNG GIRL: I can't see the beach.

FRIDAY (sings):
The island was long and narrow
Like a tall man outstretched in sleep.
The beach was white and empty.

The trees were shaking with birds.
I stood and looked up and saw a mountain all alone.
I stood and looked down and saw my friends upon the sand.

(DOCTOR, YOUNG MAN and YOUNG WOMAN hurl themselves prostrate on the beach. YOUNG MAN and YOUNG WOMAN begin to stir and recover from the sea. DOCTOR does not move.)

Four of us on the beach. But one of us, old Hookloser, who used to tell the funniest stories of them all, he was so full of water that we couldn't bring him back to life. We tried the usual spells and dances, but nothing worked.

(FRIDAY, YOUNG MAN and YOUNG WOMAN take bamboo poles and build a skeleton shelter over the man. They light a fire.)

So we built a journey house for him. And we built a fire, so we could cook and eat old Hookloser, so we could all take some of the soul of that man, who we loved, into the future with us. But we were still sharpening our knives, when death visited us again.

(CRUSOE stalks in carrying his gun, pistols in his belt. He doubles up and is almost sick. He begins to walk stealthily forward. FRIDAY, YOUNG MAN and YOUNG WOMAN see him, surprised at first, then curious. YOUNG MAN smiles and walks towards CRUSOE. CRUSOE levels musket at him. A bang, possibly made by FRIDAY on an instrument. YOUNG MAN falls, screaming, clutching chest wound, struggles, lies still.)

CRUSOE (as he fires): In the name of God the Father –

(YOUNG GIRL begins to run, freezes as gun pointed at her.)

FRIDAY: He shot Ivory first. You remember Ivory, who used to sing so loudly, and badly and happily? And Weaver, who painted the meeting poles of our meeting hut, Weaver who could move so silently when we were hunting, he ran towards the sea. But death ran after him.

(Another bang, YOUNG GIRL falls, screams, struggles, dies.)

I did not run. It was very bad.

(He crouches beside the fire.)

I put vines round my wrists to show that we were not a tribe of warriors.

(CRUSOE walks slowly over to FRIDAY, inspects the vines on his wrists, from a safe distance, pistol levelled.)

CRUSOE: What's this? A prisoner? Your poor savage.

(CRUSOE takes the vines from FRIDAY's wrists.)

I have come to rescue you from the clutches of these foul cannibals.

(CRUSOE places his foot on FRIDAY's prostrated head, poses, removes foot. Then he pokes FRIDAY to his feet with his gun.)

Here, follow me. I have saved your life.

(CRUSOE starts to walk, turns and beckons to FRIDAY.)

And what is more, I shall attempt to save your benighted soul.

(FRIDAY stares at him. CRUSOE walks back, gets behind FRIDAY, prods him with gun.)

I have changed my mind. You won't follow me. You will go first. There must be no risk. No risk at all.

(FRIDAY and CRUSOE perform a circular walk ending up outside stockade. As they pass the corpses, FRIDAY speaks to them over his shoulder.)

FRIDAY: All right, you can stop being corpses now.

(TRIBE thoughtfully return to their places in the audience. If possible the stockade has a ladder which swings over when rope is pulled. CRUSOE pulls rope, ladder swings over. CRUSOE motions FRIDAY to climb over it. FRIDAY does so, CRUSOE pulls ladder back, climbs over himself. (This can, of course, be done with one fixed ladder, but less interestingly.) FRIDAY wanders into CRUSOE's corner, inspecting the many objects which hang on the wall, touching CRUSOE's rudimentary bed. CRUSOE pulls him out of corner, indicates floor by the stockade.)

CRUSOE: No, no. Not in there. That *my* place. This your place. You sleep here. You. I can't call you *you.* Can't even give you a Christian name, seeing that you're certainly no Christian. Not yet. I know, let's see, what day of the week is it?

(CRUSOE consults a long row of notches on a pole which is part of the wall.)

Wednesday, Thursday, Friday. That'll do. You — Friday. Because I saved you on a Friday. Yes. And Friday — you

(Miming it.)

— sleep — here. Friday — sleep — here.

(FRIDAY lies down and closes his eyes. CRUSOE backs into his corner. He makes it secure with a long chain and padlock round the door. If no door, the idea of locking up and barricading should be conveyed and the chain and padlock must be used in this. CRUSOE sits on his bed, very alert, gun in hand. CRUSOE watches. Night music. TRIBE make quiet sounds of morning. Maybe some bird calls.)

FRIDAY (still with eyes shut): That night I dreamed of my dead friends. While I was asleep I dreamed of the way they lived. But when I woke up, in the first light, I dreamed of the way they died. They died suddenly, like mosquitoes when you slap them on your thigh.

(CRUSOE's eyes shut. Then he opens his eyes, shakes himself, gets up. Takes two bowls, fills them both with food. Starts to take bowls out towards FRIDAY. Remembers his gun. Tries to carry it with two bowls. Can't make it. Takes one bowl and gun out. Pushes bowl to FRIDAY, who sits up. CRUSOE goes back, fetches his bowl. Remembers stool. Goes back, fetches stool. Sits with bowl in one hand, gun under the other arm, some distance from FRIDAY. They eat.)

CRUSOE: You — Friday.

FRIDAY: Fri-day.

CRUSOE: Yes, good. Friday.

FRIDAY (nods): Friday.

(Points to CRUSOE.)

Friday?

CRUSOE (shakes head): No. Me —

(Points to self.)

Me — Master.

FRIDAY: Me, Master.

CRUSOE: No, no, no.

(Points to self.)

Master.

(Points to FRIDAY.)

Friday.

(Points to self.)

Master.

FRIDAY: Ah.

(Pointing rapidly from one to the other.)

Friday. Master. Friday. Master. Friday. Master.

CRUSOE: You're sharp, lad, you're sharp. Maybe it won't take too long to teach you English.

(CRUSOE gets up, impatient to start. Points to his head.)

Head. Head.

(FRIDAY shakes his head in disbelief. CRUSOE nods emphatically. Pointing.)

Head. Head.

(FRIDAY grins, shakes his head.)

(Pointing.) Head. Nose. Mouth. Hand. Arm. Body. Leg. Foot.

(CRUSOE looks up from pointing to his foot, sits and takes gun under his arm again.)

FRIDAY (shakes his head, pointing to his head): Baskra.

(Points to his nose.)

Logglephan.

(To his mouth.)

Omra.

(To his hand.)

Lashti.

(To his arm.)

Clyserta.

(To his body.)

Olavara.

(To his leg.)

Eegra.

(To his foot.)

Dom.

CRUSOE: Friday!

FRIDAY: Master?

CRUSOE (jabbing a finger at FRIDAY's head): Head. Head.

FRIDAY (cautiously): Baskra?

CRUSOE: No, not bloody baskra. Head. Head.

(Touches his own head, then FRIDAY's. CRUSOE raises his fist, then lowers it as FRIDAY crouches away.)

This is my island, this is Master's Island and Master is an Englishman and so this island is a part of England and so we will talk English, English. Friday will talk English too. And you'll stop speaking that black language of yours if I have to tear your tongue out by the roots.

(Pulls himself together.)

Start again.

(Pointing.)

Friday.

FRIDAY: Friday.

CRUSOE (pointing): Master.

FRIDAY: Master.

CRUSOE (pointing): Head.

FRIDAY: Ba —

(CRUSOE raises his fist.)

'Ed.

CRUSOE: Head. Head.

FRIDAY: 'ed. 'Ed.

> (They freeze. FRIDAY forward to audience.)

> Every day he taught me more of his language. It was hard. Our language is more beautiful. But our language only made him angry.

> (FRIDAY rejoins CRUSOE.)

CRUSOE (claps hands): Clap.

FRIDAY (claps hands): Clap.

CRUSOE (whistles): Whistle.

FRIDAY (whistles rather beautifully): Whistle.

CRUSOE (coughs): Cough.

FRIDAY (coughs): Cough.

CRUSOE (laughs): Laugh.

FRIDAY (laughs): Laugh.

CRUSOE (cries): Cry.

FRIDAY (cries): Cry.

CRUSOE (screams): Scream.

FRIDAY (screams): Scream.

> (The TRIBE like the game and go into a rhythmic clap, whistle, cough, laugh, cry, scream jam session, dancing and trying to get audience to join in.)

CRUSOE (when session ends): Friday is —

> (Smiles and opens hands.)

> good.

FRIDAY: Master is —

> (Smiles and opens hands.)

> good.

> (CRUSOE goes to corner to sleep. FRIDAY, whistling, picks up his fishing rod, starts to go out. Then stops, borrows CRUSOE's sunshade and hat. Parades with them, pleased. Starts to climb stockade ladder, but as he reaches the top, CRUSOE wakes and rushes out to stop him.)

CRUSOE: Friday. Hat. Sunshade.

FRIDAY (grinning, nodding): Hat. Sunshade.

CRUSOE: It's time for another lesson, Friday. A new kind of lesson.

FRIDAY (settling down on the stockade): Good. A new lesson. Good.

CRUSOE: Today we will speak only in sentences. We have learned to speak in sentences, haven't we?

FRIDAY: Good. We will speak in sentences. It is a fine day. Here is a fat fish. My face is black. We will speak in sentences. Very good.

CRUSOE: Good. Friday, listen to this sentence. That hat is mine. And listen to this one. That sunshade is mine.

FRIDAY: What is *mine*?

CRUSOE: Listen, Friday. There are many things in the world. Some of these things are for everybody. There is the sky. The sky is for Master and Friday and everybody. There is the sea. The sea is for Master and Friday and everybody. But there are other things which are for some people, but not for everybody. This island, it is for Master and Friday and nobody else. These trees and their fruit, they are for Master and Friday and nobody else. And, most important, Friday, there are other things which are for one person only and for nobody else.

FRIDAY: What can be for one person only? This is a riddle, Master. A moment. What is for one person only? A man's death? That is for him only. No, no, it is for his tribe also.

CRUSOE: It is not a riddle.

(Takes off his shoe.)

This shoe is for one person only. This shoe is for Master only. That loin-cloth is for Friday only. You can say: This loin-cloth is mine.

FRIDAY (puzzled): This loin-cloth is mine?

(Looks at it, worried.)

And that shoe is mine?

CRUSOE: No, this shoe is mine. That loin-cloth is yours. You — yours. Me — mine.

FRIDAY (understanding the linguistic side, but not the implications): Ah. The shoe is yours. The loin-cloth is mine.

CRUSOE: Very good. Now. That hat is mine.

FRIDAY: But that hat does not know it is yours. It fits Friday's head, like it fits the head of Master.

CRUSOE: But it shouldn't be on Friday's head. It is for Master only.

FRIDAY: Is there some magic in the hat? Some magic that makes it for Master only?

CRUSOE: Yes, yes. There is magic in the hat. Master's magic.

(FRIDAY takes off hat and flings it to CRUSOE, who puts it on.)

You see, Friday, mine is a word full of magic. When I tell you that something is mine, it is bad luck for you to touch it unless I take off the spell.

FRIDAY: Yes, Master.

CRUSOE (shouts): That goatskin sunshade is MINE!

(FRIDAY climbs down and hands it to him. CRUSOE holds it trium-
phantly. He reaches for his musket.)

And, Friday, this gun is mine. I have put my strongest spells upon it. This
gun is mine.

FRIDAY: Yes, Master, I know that.

DOCTOR: This Master person, his mind was very ill. Did he talk such
gibberish all the time?

FRIDAY: The answer must be yes and no. Most of the time he talked like
that. But his nonsense had a pattern to it, it wasn't random. You see, he
told me that nearly all the people of his island, England, thought the same
way.

DOCTOR: You mean he claimed to come from a whole island full of people
going about saying this is mine, this is yours.

FRIDAY: Certainly. And he said that if you didn't understand the words
mine and yours in England you were either a bad man or a mad man and
should be locked away in a hole.

GIRL: They lock people in holes?

FRIDAY: Yes. If someone takes something that is not for him, they take
him to a hole made out of stone which is called a prison. A prison is a bad
hut. It is full of bad men. And in this bad hut the bad men are fed on bad
food and are made to do things they do not want to do by other bad men
who are called jailers.

GIRL: Jailers? Do the jailers live in the bad hut too?

FRIDAY: Yes. But the jailers are rewarded with gifts by the good men who
do not live in the bad hut.

DOCTOR: But if you hide a man in a bad place, away from good people,
his mind will go bad. And if his mind is already bad, his mind will rot
away and the spirit will leave him.

FRIDAY: You speak the truth. And I think that the mind of that island,
England, must be very ill.

DOCTOR: Unless, of course, England does not exist, or only exists in the
mind of Master . . . But what did you do to try to make him well again?

FRIDAY: I allowed him to think he was teaching me. And at the same time I
tried to teach him.

(FRIDAY returns to CRUSOE. FRIDAY sits and weaves a basket –
CRUSOE takes a Bible and two sticks tied together as a Cross.)

CRUSOE: Do you understand why God does not kill the Devil? It is not
because he cannot.

FRIDAY: Because your God can do anything? Yes. So he could kill the
Devil, but he is saving him for last.

(Shouts at ground in imitation of God, wagging finger.)

You bad Devil, you just wait down there, watch what I do to the others and when I've finished with them, I'll do much worse to you.

(As himself.)

That's a mighty God you've got.

CRUSOE: I think you're beginning to understand.

FRIDAY: Are all your people God's men?

CRUSOE: I'm afraid not, Friday, there are many heretics.

FRIDAY: They do not like your God?

CRUSOE: They think they believe in God. But their God is not the true God. They believe in a strange God, a foreign God.

FRIDAY: But you say there is only one God on your island.

CRUSOE: Yes. But these heretics have invented their own God. I must warn you about these heretics, Friday, in case one day you should come to my island. They are called Roman Catholics, and they are very cunning, the Papist dogs.

FRIDAY: I do not know a dog who is cunning. But if they have invented a naughty God, that's bad.

CRUSOE: That's not all. They worship the son of the mother of God. They worship statues too. God doesn't like that at all. And they worship an old man in Rome. They worship too many things.

FRIDAY: Then the people of my island must be very bad people. We worship everything.

CRUSOE: You have many gods?

FRIDAY: We've got gods everywhere. Gods sitting by the fire, gods playing in the surf, gods riding on the backs of pigs, gods hanging upside down from palm trees. Gods in our head, we've got, gods in our fingers, gods in our feet.

CRUSOE: And what are these so-called gods like?

FRIDAY: All different.

CRUSOE: Can you see them?

FRIDAY: Some of them you can see. Sometimes.

CRUSOE (springing the theological trap): Then show me one.

(FRIDAY looks around calmly, takes a banana from a bowl, hands it to CRUSOE.)

That's not a god, it's just a banana.

FRIDAY: It's just a god, too.

CRUSOE: But how can you worship a banana?

FRIDAY: Worship any way you like. So long as you mean it, the god won't mind.

CRUSOE: But you eat bananas. How can you treat a god like that?

FRIDAY: If you eat him worshipfully, the god will be pleased.

(CRUSOE passes the banana back to FRIDAY, who puts it carefully back in the bowl.)

CRUSOE: Show me another god.

(FRIDAY points at CRUSOE.)

Ah, now you may think of me as a god. But I'm not a god at all.

FRIDAY: To yourself, I think you are not yet a god. I don't think you worship yourself as you should. But still, you are a god, whether you know it or not.

CRUSOE: Show me one more god.

(FRIDAY points to himself. CRUSOE laughs.)

FRIDAY: And what does your god look like?

CRUSOE: He is so great that he cannot be seen by mere man.

FRIDAY: Well, what would he look like if man had great eyes?

CRUSOE: Let's see. He made us in his image. Therefore, he'd look like a human being.

FRIDAY: Like me, or like you?

CRUSOE: If I could see him, I suppose he'd look like me. But if you could see him, perhaps he'd look like you. Only greater of course.

FRIDAY: So your one single all alone God is really many gods?

CRUSOE: Perhaps he is one God with many shapes.

FRIDAY (thoughtfully): And perhaps one of those shapes is the shape of a banana.

(CRUSOE speechless, puts away his Cross.)

But it is bad to think only of the gods. Tell me, what is England?

CRUSOE: A great island.

FRIDAY: Friday's home is a great island too.

CRUSOE: But England is a very very great island.

FRIDAY: How many days of walking from one end to the other? Friday's island is two days and two nights long and half a day wide.

CRUSOE: A sturdy man might walk the length of England in fifty days and nights. Or perhaps forty days and nights. Or twenty days and nights upon a horse.

FRIDAY: What is a horse?

CRUSOE: A horse is — a horse is as big as ten pigs. He can carry a man on his back for many miles, many hours.

FRIDAY: And does the horse like to carry the man?

CRUSOE: God made the horse to carry us.

FRIDAY: So, when a man wants to be carried, he walks into the jungle of England and chooses a horse as big as ten pigs.

CRUSOE: No. The horse must be taught to carry the man.

FRIDAY: Does not the God of England teach the horse?

CRUSOE: And England has no jungles. Many trees, but no jungles.

FRIDAY: But, Master, a jungle is many trees.

CRUSOE: No. A jungle is hot and wet. England is cold and wet. So we have woods, not jungles. The woods are too cold for monkeys. Too cold to bear fruit.

FRIDAY: Then where do the people of England find their bananas?

CRUSOE: There are no bananas in England.

(FRIDAY laughs uproariously.)

FRIDAY: An island without bananas! Your England is a poor country.

CRUSOE: Friday, I forbid you to laugh at England.

FRIDAY: I am sorry, Master.

CRUSOE: There is nothing funny about England.

FRIDAY: No bananas! So the island must be poor.

CRUSOE: No, England is very rich. We have many things which Friday's island does not have.

FRIDAY: What things?

CRUSOE: We have coal.

FRIDAY: Is coal good?

CRUSOE: Coal is very good.

FRIDAY: Please explain coal?

CRUSOE: Coal is a black rock under the ground. Men dig it out of the ground. Then it is sold to other men.

FRIDAY: And the men who do not dig the coal eat the coal?

CRUSOE: No. They burn it.

FRIDAY: Ah. And then they eat it?

CRUSOE: No. The coal burns very slowly and gives great heat in the huts of the people. And it is good for cooking meat. Because it burns more slowly than wood, and gives more heat. And mine is a cold island.

FRIDAY: I would rather have a warm island with bananas.

CRUSOE: Let me tell you this, Friday. That my island is such a great island that greedy men sail for many days across the sea to try to take it with guns. But we are a brave island too, and we meet them with guns. And so far, thanks to the help of God, we have always beaten them away from our shores.

FRIDAY: But do your tribes always argue with guns?

CRUSOE: Nations, not tribes. Oh, we have friendly arguments as well. We have sport.

FRIDAY: What is sport?

CRUSOE: Sport is . . . sport is war without weapons and battles without bloodshed. But it's more than that. It involves values like chivalry and sportsmanship. These are complicated beliefs and it takes many years in a special school to learn them. Sport — sport is cut-throat competition in which no throats are cut.

FRIDAY: I think I will never understand. We have no such special schools on Friday's island. We have no schools at all.

CRUSOE (putting his hand on FRIDAY's shoulder): I know. I'll show you. I'll show you what sport is all about.

(CRUSOE brings out a little platform with two levels made out of boxes. On top of the platform is a cup made out of a coconut.)

First we'll run what is called a race. I will say ready, steady, go and when I say go, we will both start to run towards that post.

(CRUSOE points to the end of the hall.)

And then we'll see who is the winner.

FRIDAY: Winner?

CRUSOE: The best runner.

FRIDAY: The fastest runner.

CRUSOE: Yes . . . well, but the important thing is not whether you win or lose.

FRIDAY: Then what is important?

CRUSOE: The important thing is how you play — the important thing is *how* you run.

FRIDAY: Good. I see. I understand.

CRUSOE: Right. Ready? Steady? Go!

(CRUSOE runs desperately, while FRIDAY lopes along in an easy, flowing style, but somewhat more slowly. CRUSOE wins and, puffing heavily, doubled up, waits at the winning post. FRIDAY glides up.)

You let me win. You weren't trying.

FRIDAY: *You* won?

CRUSOE: I got here first.

FRIDAY: But you said the important thing is how you run. I ran very beautifully.

(To TRIBE.)

Didn't I? I enjoyed every step along the sand. You did not seem to like the running. Your body was jerking and not happy. And listen to what your breathing is saying. Your breathing is not saying: thank you, that was good running. Your breathing says: hey, that hurt, what do you think you're doing to me?

CRUSOE: Friday, as you say, you didn't got to a sportsmanship school. Perhaps that view of sport is too sophisticated. Forget what I said before. The important thing is to win. Take football.

(CRUSOE produces goalposts. CRUSOE and FRIDAY face each other. A football made of rolled up cloth between them.)

TRIBE: Fri-day.

(Clap clap clap.)

Fri-day.

(Clap clap clap. And other good football crowd noises as appropriate.)

CRUSOE: Remember now, it's not how you play, but whether you can get that ball through that goal. But you must not touch the ball with your hands. I will kick off.

(CRUSOE kicks off. FRIDAY stands aside and lets him run right up to his goal and kick it through. CRUSOE runs back with the ball, puffing angrily.)

Why didn't you stop me? You're meant to stop me.

FRIDAY: I am playing this game very carefully. I have a plan. The first part of the plan is to let you wear yourself out. This part of the plan is almost complete.

CRUSOE: Your kick-off. What is the second part of your plan?

(FRIDAY kicks off. The ball zooms down the hall into CRUSOE's goal. CRUSOE runs back to retrieve it, returns puffing more than ever.)

FRIDAY: Goal!

CRUSOE: One all, I suppose. But that was, I'd say, a combination of brute strength and very good luck.

FRIDAY: No, not really. I concentrated one part of my spirit in my right foot, one part of my spirit in the ball and one part of my spirit in the goal. And then I drew the three parts of my spirit together.

CRUSOE: You did, did you! Look, I don't pray to my God over a football match. If I did, no doubt he'd pack my goal-mouth with archangels. So don't use your heathen magic. Or your hands for that matter. My kick-off now. Third goal settles the match.

(CRUSOE kicks off, trying to get the rebound from FRIDAY's feet, but

FRIDAY's feet are suddenly dancing behind and at each side of the ball, tap-dancing almost. FRIDAY side-steps CRUSOE, waits for him to come in again, waits, side-steps and is heading for CRUSOE's goal when CRUSOE tackles him from behind, tripping him. FRIDAY recovers, indignant. The TRIBE jeer.)

All right, unfair tackle. Free kick to you.

(FRIDAY stares at him. Approaches the ball. FRIDAY bends down, picks up the ball between his teeth, runs to CRUSOE's goal, this time sprinting like mad, pops ball in goal and then dances round goal-posts. CRUSOE comes puffing up.)

That's not allowed. Teeth aren't allowed.

FRIDAY: You never told me.

CRUSOE: It's obvious, isn't it? It's football, not teethball.

FRIDAY: Where's the rule against it?

CRUSOE: It's never been done.

FRIDAY: Where's the rule?

(They begin to wag fingers at each other. DOCTOR separates them. They recover. Drum rolls. CRUSOE mounts top of platform. FRIDAY on lower level of platform, holding the cup.)

CRUSOE: First the award for the winner of the one hundred yards sprint. First, Master. Second, Friday.

(FRIDAY proffers the cup, which CRUSOE takes with a nod. CRUSOE holds it proudly.)

And now, my national anthem. After the presentation, we have to sing the winner's national anthem. You know, the one I taught you, God Save? Right.

(CRUSOE and FRIDAY sing, FRIDAY muttering somewhat.)

CRUSOE and FRIDAY (sing as band beats out rhythm):
> God save our gracious King
> Long live our noble King
> God save the King.
> Send him victorious
> Happy and glorious
> Long to reign over us!
> God save our King.

FRIDAY: And now for the football prize.

(FRIDAY jumps on to top platform. CRUSOE edges down to second level.)

And now the glorious award for the great football battle without bloodshed. The score: Friday — two. Master — one.

(CRUSOE proffers cup, which FRIDAY takes. FRIDAY sings and dances on his platform.)

(Sings.)

> Let me tell you of a war in which there was no fighting.
> Let me tell you of a battle in which there was no hurting.
> Victory did not matter at all, it did not matter,
> And yet nothing mattered but the victory.
> How you fought was the important thing,
> And yet how you fought was not important at all.
> Let me tell you of the triumph of Friday
> In the great war of football . . .

(CRUSOE stomps off in a huff.)

YOUNG MAN (thoughtfully): Perhaps there are some good things about this Master.

DOCTOR (automatically): When meat goes bad, it becomes poison.

YOUNG MAN: That's an old saying. But there is more to a man than his meat.

DOCTOR: I am wrong. You are right. And so, tell us what is good about this Master?

YOUNG MAN: Perhaps this idea of sport is good. Perhaps running against each other would be good.

YOUNG GIRL: Why run against each other? Why not run together?

DOCTOR: Yes, why not run with each other, as we have always done?

YOUNG MAN: No, listen. Suppose that every year, our whole tribe should meet on a long beach. There would be a signal, then we would run to the other end of the beach. And the one who ran the fastest, he would receive a prize.

(The rest of the TRIBE fall about with laughter.)

YOUNG GIRL: What sort of prize?

YOUNG MAN: A pig, perhaps.

YOUNG GIRL: Why run for a pig? The pigs lie around all day in their compound just out there. If you want some pork, there it is.

YOUNG MAN: Forget the prize then. But it would be good to find out which of the tribe could run the fastest. He could be paid some honour by the tribe. He could be called the Runner.

YOUNG GIRL: If you like, we will call you the Runner. Just like that. We will call you any name you choose.

YOUNG MAN: No, I would like to know who is really the fastest. And it would be good for the tribe. We would all practise running. And so we would move more quickly when we're hunting. Or when we are attacked.

DOCTOR (to GIRL): I think this boy is not very well. Will you take him to his hut and make him better?

(YOUNG GIRL smiles and takes YOUNG MAN's hand. He shakes her off.)

YOUNG MAN: But I'm not —

(GIRL takes his hand again, still smiling.)

DOCTOR: You are not very well. Come back when you are better.

(YOUNG MAN allows himself to be led out.)

FRIDAY: Master would have recommended bathing in a cold river.

(FRIDAY walks around, takes bow and arrow, watches, aims, shoots, picks up dead bird. Dead bird in his hand, clambers over the ladder into the stockade. He sees CRUSOE, shirtless, a small branch over his shoulder. CRUSOE starts guiltily, throws down the branch, pulls on his shirt awkwardly. FRIDAY thoughtfully hangs the bird on the top of the stockade, then leans against a post and folds his arms.)

Should I not have come back, Master? Your eyes are angry.

(CRUSOE sits down, knees up in front of him, hugging them.)

CRUSOE: No, no, I'm not angry. Well, I'm not angry with you, Friday.

FRIDAY (picking up the branch): You are angry with the stick?

CRUSOE: No, Friday. God is angry with me. And so I'm angry with myself.

FRIDAY: That's serious, Master. How do you know God is angry?

CRUSOE: Because I had a dream.

FRIDAY: A dream about God? That is lucky.

CRUSOE: No. A dream about a woman. About the body of a woman.

FRIDAY: A love dream? But surely God will not send a love dream if he's angry with you?

CRUSOE: Not love. It was lust. And in this dream I used this woman. Like an animal.

FRIDAY: You killed her?

CRUSOE: I copulated with her.

FRIDAY: Couldn't she do it well? Didn't you enjoy it?

CRUSOE: I was very happy. Happy. Till I woke up. And then I was ashamed. And I knew God was angry. And so I was beating myself with the branch. So that God would forgive me.

(FRIDAY examines the branch.)

FRIDAY: No, I still can't understand your God. Why should he be angry? I am sometimes angry, Master, but I am angry if someone hurts me. You have not hurt your God. You have only hurt your own back.

CRUSOE: Every time we surrender to the temptations of the flesh, the agony of Jesus on the Cross is increased one hundredfold.

FRIDAY: Why?

CRUSOE: Because he bears our sins. He takes them on himself.

FRIDAY: And our sins hurt him?

CRUSOE: He is in great pain, Friday.

FRIDAY: And he takes all our badness?

CRUSOE: Yes.

FRIDAY: And yet he is not bad at all.

CRUSOE: Not at all.

FRIDAY: Help me to understand. Show me, Master. Pretend that you are God. And pretend that I am Master.

CRUSOE: I'll pretend no such thing. I couldn't be God.

FRIDAY: Unless you show me, Master, I shall never understand.

(CRUSOE stands up, walks up and down, deliberating, stops suddenly.)

CRUSOE: All right, Friday. You must be taught. You are now — Master. I shall be God.

(CRUSOE climbs to the top of the ladder and sits there.)

You are Master, and I am God and I am watching over you always.

FRIDAY (walking like CRUSOE, sings):
Poor Master, Poor Master
I have walked alone
For many, many years.

Poor Master, poor Master
I have slept alone
For many, many years.

CRUSOE: But you are not alone. I am God and I am with you always.

FRIDAY: Oh yes. Thank you, God. I feel tired, God. I am going to bed. I go to my bed alone. Good night, God.

CRUSOE: Good night, poor Robinson Crusoe.

(FRIDAY lies down and pulls goatskin over him. He shuts his eyes and pretends to snore. CRUSOE stares at him from his perch. FRIDAY sits up suddenly.)

FRIDAY: You must tell me the dream or I cannot dream it.

CRUSOE: It was a wicked dream.

FRIDAY: You must tell me, or I cannot understand what is wicked.

CRUSOE: I will tell you.

(FRIDAY nods, and lies down as before.)

I dreamed a dream and in that dream a woman came and touched my skin.

(FRIDAY touches his own skin without opening his eyes.)

She laid my head upon her breasts. She touched my ears.

(FRIDAY touches his own ears.)

I said, why? Why? She said: because your ears are beautiful.

FRIDAY (as if sleep-talking): Why? Why? Because your ears are beautiful.

CRUSOE (more intensely): Her clothes, she wore clothes, but they had no more substance than moonlight. Her body moved over mine like waves moving over the sand.

(FRIDAY moves his body in response to waves.)

I began to jabber and thrust with love.

(FRIDAY tosses his body and jabbers nonsense.)

Stop! Stop it!

(FRIDAY sits up.)

And then I woke up and I said to God: God, I am vile. Take my life for there is no health in me.

FRIDAY: God, I am vile. Take my life, for there is no health in me.

CRUSOE: And then God said to me: yes, you are a creature of vileness. A night-monster. A scarlet snake. Take that branch and chastise thyself that thou may sin no more.

FRIDAY (standing up): God said that?

CRUSOE: Something like that.

FRIDAY: So you took the branch?

CRUSOE: I am God's servant.

FRIDAY: Oh, but Master, you're not alone on this island. I'm here. If you'd told me that you needed loving, I would have helped you.

CRUSOE: Helped me?

FRIDAY: I have a body too. I am a loving man.

CRUSOE: Down on your knees, down on your knees. Master is vile, but you, you —

(FRIDAY falls to his knees.)

FRIDAY: Is it bad to love?

CRUSOE: Man shall not love man. Man shall not love man.

(CRUSOE climbs down from his perch into the stockade, more gently.)

Friday, you are only a savage and you understand little. But you have offered me a very bad gift. A poisonous gift. And you must be punished. As you have spoken like a beast, you shall be, just for today, a beast.

Everywhere we go today, you shall crawl upon your hands and knees.

FRIDAY (going down on his hands and knees): It will please your God? He will feel better?

CRUSOE: God may forgive you.

(CRUSOE walks, with musket and sunshade. FRIDAY crawls on all fours behind him. CRUSOE stops, takes pot-shot at bird, misses. FRIDAY catches up, tugs at his breeches for attention. CRUSOE turns rapidly, steps back.)

What is it?

FRIDAY: Master, I have a thought.

CRUSOE: Oh, you've been thinking have you? Makes a change.

(Sits.)

I am all attention. Master is listening. Tell me your great thought.

FRIDAY: I think this island is not a good island. Not good for Master. Not good for Friday.

CRUSOE: Why? God in his mercy saved both our lives by placing this island where it is.

FRIDAY: But there is not enough on this island.

CRUSOE: Not enough what?

FRIDAY: Not enough love.

CRUSOE: So what do you suggest? That we should pray for a shipload of women to be shipwrecked on the beach?

FRIDAY: We should leave the island. We should build a boat and leave the island.

CRUSOE: Leave the — but where could we go? I've tried, Friday, during the years before you came, I tried over and over again. I kept signal fires burning to attract passing ships. But no ships passed. And I could find no way of building a craft that would take me for a journey of more than a few days. I'm no shipwright. And nor are you. And the journey from here to any British port would take us months, through storms and unknown currents.

FRIDAY: But Friday's island is only two days and two nights away. I know the course to set.

CRUSOE: But a ship would take us all our time to build. And there's hunting to be done, wild pigs to be caught. There's fishing, there's drainage, repairs to the hut, clothes to be mended — there's no time to build a boat.

FRIDAY: But I do all those tasks. And while I do them, you could build a boat.

CRUSOE: Suppose I did. Suppose I did build a raft and it would carry us to your island, eh? I know what would happen. Your cannibal friends would eat me.

FRIDAY: No, no.

CRUSOE: But on the beach. That day when I rescued you. They were eating a man.

FRIDAY: Yes, they were. But he drowned when our canoe was wrecked. And when one of our people is killed by an accident or by the warriors of another tribe, we honour his soul by eating him. So that his soul lives in us.

CRUSOE: You mean you don't deliberately kill people so you can eat them?

FRIDAY: When people try to kill us, we kill them. But we would not honour them by eating them. The tribe may only eat the people of the tribe.

CRUSOE: So they would treat me well. They wouldn't honour me by serving me up with a tomato in my mouth.

FRIDAY: You would be treated as a guest.

CRUSOE: And perhaps I could teach them?

FRIDAY: I think they would learn many things from you, Master.

CRUSOE: Two days' and two nights' journey . . . perhaps. Friday, I'm making no promises, but if I have any spare time in the next few years, I will make a seaworthy craft that shall carry us to your home . . . perhaps.

(FRIDAY, overwhelmed, grabs CRUSOE's foot and starts to kiss it. CRUSOE, embarrassed, withdraws foot. He stares at FRIDAY. Then, outraged at being touched so intimately, he kicks FRIDAY and walks away. YOUNG MAN and GIRL return, both smiling.)

DOCTOR: You're confusing me. Did he want love or didn't he?

FRIDAY (getting up): He didn't want it from me. He wanted everything from me except my love.

(CRUSOE sits in his corner, surrounded by his many possessions. He is reading a Bible. FRIDAY rings ship's bell that hangs beside CRUSOE's door. CRUSOE shuts Bible and takes his musket on his lap.)

CRUSOE: Friend or foe?

FRIDAY (outside): Friday, Master.

CRUSOE (putting aside musket): Come in.

(FRIDAY comes in. CRUSOE motions him to sit on the floor, FRIDAY sits.)

You're back early this morning, Friday. Working fast today? Washed out all the pans? Lit the signal fire? Caught plenty of fish? Or were you going after the goats today?

FRIDAY (shaking his head): I've been swimming.

CRUSOE: Good, good, trying to salvage some more treasure from that old wreck, eh?

FRIDAY: No, Master, I've been swimming because I like to swim. My body agrees with the ocean.

CRUSOE: But what about your duties, Friday? Your jobs? You know what I keep telling you. It's all very well to talk about your rights, all very well. But what about your responsibilities, eh?

FRIDAY: I am not doing responsibilities today, Master. I am doing rights.

CRUSOE: And what about the fish? What are we going to eat tonight?

FRIDAY: The fish tell me that they will come if Master calls them.

CRUSOE: Friday, it's your job to fish. And the signal fire, what about the signal fire?

FRIDAY: The signal fire says that Master may light it whenever he chooses.

CRUSOE: But, Friday, that's another of your little tasks.

FRIDAY: No, Master. It is Master's turn to work.

CRUSOE: You think I don't work? You accuse me of not working? How do you suppose we'd survive on this island if it wasn't for me?

FRIDAY: Friday fishes, Friday hunts, Friday lights the fires, Friday cooks, Friday mends the clothes —

CRUSOE: And he does all those things very well indeed. You have a good hunting eye and supple muscles, so you work with your eyes and with your body. But I am Master, and I work with my brain.

FRIDAY: Has your brain built a raft yet?

CRUSOE: I'm working it out. I'm working it out on paper.

FRIDAY: A raft of paper?

CRUSOE (angry): I'M WORKING IT OUT! Listen. Who has the burden of making all the decisions on this island? Who has to say when we shall eat and when we shall refrain from eating? Who is responsible for assigning tasks, for maintaining morale? Who decides, with the help of God Almighty, what is wrong and what is right?

FRIDAY: I would like to try to do that work, Master.

CRUSOE: No, no, Friday. That is Master's work.

FRIDAY: And so Friday is just one of Master's possessions. Like his sunshade. Like those slaves you told me about.

CRUSOE: That's unkind and ungrateful, Friday. I don't look on you as a slave.

FRIDAY: Then what am I?

CRUSOE: You are an ignorant savage.

(Calming.)

I'm just trying to teach you, Friday. You are a man who works with me. Willingly. For the common good.

FRIDAY: I am willing to share all Master's work. But I have decided that I will not do all the work.

(CRUSOE picks up his musket.)

Yes. The gun is yours, Master. I know the gun.

(Takes the barrel and presses it to his head.)

I have decided, Master. I will not live as a slave. You may kill me.

CRUSOE (standing, holding musket): If I kill you, I'm only doing it for your own good.

FRIDAY: Surely. Because you have often told me how it has saved your mind to have another human being on the island. And since, when you kill me, you will be all alone on the island, all alone in the world, I know you are not killing me for pleasure.

CRUSOE: Let go of the gun.

FRIDAY: When you kill me, I would like to be killed well. I think that if the gun points to this part of my head, where my spirit lives, I will die very quickly. So let me hold the gun.

CRUSOE: I'm not going to kill you.

(FRIDAY lets go of the gun slowly. CRUSOE puts it down.)

FRIDAY: And I'm not working today.

CRUSOE: Come on, Friday, be reasonable.

FRIDAY: I'm not working.

CRUSOE: Shut your eyes.

FRIDAY: You *are* going to kill me.

CRUSOE: No, no, shut your eyes.

(FRIDAY shuts his eyes. CRUSOE finds box under his bed, brings out a handful of gold coins, hides box again.)

Open your eyes. Look, Friday, if you will do all the fishing and firelighting and other jobs, just as before, I will pay you. And then you cannot call yourself a slave. For the difference between a free man and a slave is that a free man is paid wages.

FRIDAY: But what are these wages?

CRUSOE (holding out handful of coins): At the end of every week, when you have done all your work, Master will give you one of these for each day. They are called coins. They are good magic. Look.

(CRUSOE hands FRIDAY a coin.)

FRIDAY: It is pretty. It is cold. But what do you use it for?

CRUSOE: It's no use at all, not in itself. But it is good to have.

FRIDAY: Why?

CRUSOE: That is a coin. You work for a week. I give you a coin. You keep the coin. It is yours. At the end of the next week's work I give you another coin. Soon you have many many coins. And if you come to me and say — Master, I would like that brass kettle on the wall —

FRIDAY: You will say: no, the brass kettle is mine.

CRUSOE: No, not if you have coins. I will say this: if you give me three of your coins, you may have that brass kettle.

FRIDAY: I don't need a kettle.

CRUSOE: That's just an example. Suppose you want my lamp, which I made myself. That would be, let's say, four coins.

FRIDAY: I see. So I can bring you coins, and you will give me kettles and lamps.

CRUSOE: If you bring enough coins, Friday, you will be able to buy anything.

FRIDAY: Anything . . . for different things, I must give you different numbers of coins?

CRUSOE: That's right.

(Like a shopkeeper.)

This saw for instance, this excellent saw, I might let you have it for three coins. Now this bag of nails might be one coin. Should you fancy some sugar, I could let you have a small bag for only two coins. A knife and fork would be three coins for the pair. A good shirt, finely embroidered, very rare, I could let that go at six coins. A home-made clay pot, well, it's not perfect, let's say two pots, no three pots for two coins. And you'll need a seaman's chest to keep all these things in. Well, a seaman's chest will last you a lifetime, that would be ten coins, ten at least.

FRIDAY: But I use all these things anyway, when I need them. Why do I have to give you coins now?

CRUSOE: Because you are a free man. You insisted on freedom, but with freedom comes responsibility.

FRIDAY: But I don't really want any of those things.

CRUSOE: You mean to tell me that you don't want a ship's hammock, going for only eleven coins?

FRIDAY: I sleep best on the earth.

CRUSOE: How about a sword, just a little rusty, but excellent for pig-sticking? Twenty coins.

FRIDAY: No.

CRUSOE: Isn't there anything you want?

FRIDAY: Perhaps so. But for the moment I will keep my coins. How many of these coins would I have to pay you for your whole hut and everything in it?

CRUSOE (laughs): You're a rascal, Friday.

FRIDAY: How much?

CRUSOE: It is a joke, isn't it?

FRIDAY: Yes, a joke. If I bought everything you have —

(Laughs.)

— you'd have to work for me, and I'd have to give you coins so you could buy everything back again.

CRUSOE: The hut and everything in it . . . I think I'd settle for two thousand coins.

FRIDAY: Two thousand coins . . . that's fair.

(CRUSOE and FRIDAY shake hands, both laughing.)

DOCTOR (laughing): Your story's too absurd. I don't believe a word of it.

FRIDAY: You are seventy years old, and you still don't know that all true stories are absurd?

DOCTOR: But this Master was in a very extreme condition. This fantasy that a man should work all day for the sake of a little shining disc of metal . . .

YOUNG MAN: Perhaps you thought it best to let Master play out his fantasies in real life?

FRIDAY: That was one reason for playing his games. But I had other reasons too.

(On bed CRUSOE sits. FRIDAY stands in front of him. Box of coins on bed.)

CRUSOE: And so, here are your wages for your first week of work as a truly free man. One two three four five six.

FRIDAY: Seven? Seven days in a week.

CRUSOE: But the seventh is Sunday. You don't work on a Sunday.

FRIDAY: I cook on Sunday.

CRUSOE: But you can't be paid for Sunday . . . Unless . . . All right, here you are, that's seven — but only on condition that you put one coin in the collection box when I hold the service every Sunday.

FRIDAY: But, Master —

CRUSOE: I'm a fair man, Friday. I'll set the church money aside. And when I've got enough I'll use it to pay you extra money to build a chapel.

(FRIDAY turns to go, coins in hand.)

And from now on, Friday, you will pay for your education.

(FRIDAY goes outside the stockade. He takes a talking drum, the kind that changes its note as you squeeze the strings along its side. As he walks along the wet sand, he begins to play the drum and dance to its rhythms. CRUSOE joins him and sits reading his Bible.)

FRIDAY (chants):

> The sun can cook an island
> But the moon cannot even boil an egg.
>
> Nobody teaches the shark to swim
> But the monkey never learns.
>
> The wind can tear a forest down
> But the tallest tree cannot harm the wind.
>
> The body of Friday can show its happiness
> But Master can only smile with half his mouth.

(CRUSOE jumps to his feet and comes over.)

CRUSOE: You're trying to make me lose my temper.

(FRIDAY stops dancing.)

FRIDAY: I think you need to lose something.

CRUSOE: Master.

FRIDAY: You need to lose something, Master. Why don't you ever dance?

(FRIDAY starts to dance again.)

CRUSOE: You want me to dance so that you can laugh at me.

FRIDAY: I think you should dance, Master. Good for the body, good for the spirit.

CRUSOE: You'd laugh at me.

FRIDAY: I might laugh, Master, if you make a funny dance. I laugh at funny dancing.

CRUSOE: And bad dancing?

FRIDAY: There's nothing funny about bad dancing.

CRUSOE: No. I'm not going to dance.

FRIDAY: Come, it is so easy. Even the grass can dance. Dance for me, and I'll give you a coin.

CRUSOE (laughing): Right, Friday, it's a deal. Give me your drum.

(FRIDAY, smiling, hands over the drum. CRUSOE experiments with it, then, humming to himself, begins to move into a stiff dance.)

FRIDAY: No, you're not dancing yet.

CRUSOE (continuing): I'm dancing.

FRIDAY: You're not dancing at all. Only your feet are dancing.

CRUSOE (continuing): What am I supposed to dance with?

FRIDAY: Dance with your whole body. Dance with your whole spirit.

(CRUSOE earnestly tries to do this, but it's still stiff and he knows it. Suddenly he stops and hands the drum back. FRIDAY gives him a coin.)

You are starting to dance. But you must practise, you must practise until you dance as naturally as a two-year-old child. Observe the trees and how they grow. And now, Master, make me a song.

CRUSOE: That I won't do. Not for love nor money. I don't make songs. In England songs are only made by riff-raff.

FRIDAY: Riff-raff, riff-raff — is that a song?

CRUSOE: No, riff-raff is a class of person.

FRIDAY (nods): Ah, another class. You have told me of the classes. Riff-raff. I think I am riff-raff. This riff-raff is a class of song-makers?

CRUSOE: You could say that. But who makes the songs on your island?

FRIDAY: Everybody. We are all riff-raff, you see. Somebody needs a song, he makes it. Of course, some make better songs than others. But, Master, sing one of the songs made by your riff-raff.

CRUSOE: I've got a terrible voice.

FRIDAY: Not always. It is sometimes a good voice.

CRUSOE: But I don't sing. Except when I'm alone. Sometimes.

FRIDAY: But, Master, you are alone.

CRUSOE: Almost. Almost. Friday, I will sing you a song. Won't sing it well. But I'll do my best. You play your drum.

FRIDAY: A riff-raff song.

(FRIDAY accompanies CRUSOE with his drum.)

CRUSOE (slowly and with much feeling):
>    It was a lover and his lass,
>    With a hey, and a ho, and a hey nonino,
>    That o'er the green corn-field did pass
>    In spring-time, the only pretty ring-time,
>    When birds do sing, hey ding a ding ding,
>    Sweet lovers love the spring.
>
>    Between the acres of the rye,
>    With a hey, and a ho, and a hey nonino,
>    These pretty country-folks would lie
>    In spring-time, the only pretty ring-time
>    When birds do sing, hey ding a ding ding,
>    Sweet lovers —

(CRUSOE, much moved by the song, beats his head on the ground. FRIDAY stops him.)

FRIDAY: I like your song, Master, if you want to kill yourself, that is not the best way.

CRUSOE: Not trying — to kill myself. Kill my desires. Killing myself would be — a crime — before God.

FRIDAY: And what will God say about the way you kill your desires?

CRUSOE: He will rejoice.

FRIDAY: He is a frightening God, your God.

CRUSOE: He's meant to be a frightening God.

(Silence. FRIDAY looks around.)

FRIDAY: Hey, you've been working on that raft!

CRUSOE: Yes. Almost ready. Needs sails yet.

FRIDAY: But does it float?

CRUSOE: I — of course it floats.

FRIDAY: I'll try it.

(TRIBE carry on raft.)

CRUSOE: It's a good raft, isn't it?

FRIDAY: I've never been on a raft before —

(FRIDAY mounts raft, is lifted by TRIBE.)

Here I go. It's floating. I'm floating too — it carries me.

CRUSOE: Told you it would.

FRIDAY (singing and dancing):
    I am going to ride to the island of Friday.
    All the tribe will be waiting on the beach.
    There'll be singing and weeping.
    There'll be dancing and laughter —

(TRIBE, who have been singing along, tip FRIDAY off raft.)

It doesn't even carry me. It won't take both of us.

CRUSOE: It'll take some time to put right.

FRIDAY: I could help.

CRUSOE: You have your work to do, Friday. And I have mine. Perhaps God means that we should stay on this island forever. We must not think only of the raft. We must also try to make ourselves better men.

FRIDAY: I thought we did quite a lot of that.

CRUSOE: Not enough, Friday, not enough. We've been very slack. Come with me.

(They return to inside stockade.)

Sit.

(FRIDAY sits on ground. CRUSOE produces blackboard, hooks it onto wall. Then he puts black gown over his shoulders and takes a long stick in his hand.)

FRIDAY: Are you going to show me magic today, Master?

CRUSOE: There is no such thing as magic.

(FRIDAY grins ruefully.)

Sit down, today we make a fresh start.

(FRIDAY sits down, shifts to make himself comfortable.)

FRIDAY: Every day we make a fresh start. Every day I'm a new Friday and you're a new Master.

CRUSOE (angry): That's what I mean. That's exactly what I mean.

FRIDAY: You are angry, Master? Are your bowels unhappy? I dried those blue herbs. They'll make you happy again. I'll fetch them. They're drying in —

CRUSOE: Sit down! My bowels are perfectly happy. Sit down and listen. Friday, I have been trying to teach you. I've been trying to turn you into a civilized human being.

FRIDAY: I think you're doing very well, Master, I feel more civilized every day. The more we talk, the more civilized I feel.

CRUSOE: And the more you talk, the angrier I get.

FRIDAY: I don't try to make you angry. I try to help. But if you feel angry, please do not hide your anger.

CRUSOE: That's enough. Listen. Listen. When I started to teach you, I made allowances. Maybe I shouldn't have done that, maybe it's all my fault.

FRIDAY: Don't blame yourself. Not for anything.

CRUSOE: Don't patronize me! I'm not blaming myself. Listen. I decided that since I was teaching a savage, I should allow him to ask as many questions as he liked, to talk back at me as much as he liked, even to make fun of me now and then.

FRIDAY: I laugh when I feel a joke. I don't know what else to do with a joke.

CRUSOE: You feel too many jokes. But now I've decided to do something drastic. From now on, every day when you return from the morning hunt, there will be a teaching time.

FRIDAY: Good, good, I want to learn.

CRUSOE: But teaching time will be different from our old talking times. I will do the talking, because I am the teacher.

FRIDAY: And if I —

CRUSOE: And if you want to talk, you will raise your hand. And if I want you to talk I will observe that your hand is raised and I will say: Yes, Friday, what did you want to say? And only then will you be permitted to talk.

(FRIDAY raises his hand.)

No, not now. I haven't even started.

(FRIDAY keeps his hand raised.)

Put your hand down.

(FRIDAY lowers hand.)

You will put your hand up only when it is absolutely necessary. Only when there is something that you do not understand.

(FRIDAY puts hand up.)

Put it down. The lesson has not yet begun.

(FRIDAY lowers hand.)

Today I am going to teach you about education.

(Writes 'EDUCATION' on the board.)

E-D-U-C-A-T-I-O-N. Education. From the Latin – Duco, I lead. I lead.

(FRIDAY's hand is up again.)

Good question. What is Latin? Latin is a language which was spoken by the Romans.

(FRIDAY, who has lowered his hand, shoots it up again.)

Yes. The Romans were people who many years ago lived in Italy. Italy is a big country near England which is shaped like a boot. The Romans had a great deal of Education.

(Points to word on board. FRIDAY's hand again.)

Yes, Friday . . .

(Very deliberately.)

What did you want to say?

FRIDAY: The Romans *used* to live in Italy, shaped like a boot?

CRUSOE: Correct.

FRIDAY: And where do the Romans live now?

CRUSOE: The Romans are all dead now. That's not the point about the Romans. The Romans had a great deal of ED-U-CA-TION. And they gave us this word. I will now explain this word.

FRIDAY: I am sorry about the Romans.

CRUSOE: You didn't raise your hand. Take care, Friday, take care. The first principle of education is this. There is a teacher. That's me. Who leads. Duco. I lead. And there is a pupil. That's you. And you follow.

(FRIDAY's hand up.)

Yes?

FRIDAY: What if the teacher loses his way?

CRUSOE: The teacher knows the way. And if he does not always know the way by heart, he has many books which show him the way.

FRIDAY: These are magic books?

CRUSOE: If you forget to put up your hand again, Friday, you will be punished.

(FRIDAY's hand up again.)

FRIDAY: What is punished? Is it a principle of education?

CRUSOE (deep breath): Punished. It is not only a principle of education, it is a principle of life. It means to hurt someone because they have done something bad. It is not my invention. God punishes. If we live a bad life, then, when we are dead, God punishes us. But a teacher cannot wait until his pupil is dead, so a teacher punishes as soon as a pupil is bad.

FRIDAY: But how does he punish?

CRUSOE: Friday, you didn't put up your hand. Friday, that is very bad. You will now be punished.

FRIDAY: Ah.

CRUSOE: Stand up. Hold out your hand.

(FRIDAY obeys. CRUSOE brings down his stick across FRIDAY's hand. FRIDAY grabs the stick, wrests it away and breaks it in two.)

Friday, that is very wrong. You must learn to take your punishment like a man.

FRIDAY: I am a man. Look, if someone does a bad thing to someone else, they are punished. Is that right?

CRUSOE: Yes.

FRIDAY: Well, the stick did a bad thing to my hand. So my hand punished the stick.

CRUSOE: Pick up the pieces.

(FRIDAY looks at him for a second, then picks up the pieces of stick. FRIDAY looks at the pieces of stick in his hand.)

FRIDAY (to the stick): You must learn to take your punishment like a stick.

(CRUSOE takes off gown.)

YOUNG GIRL: He was a very bad pupil that Master.

FRIDAY: I kept trying – Look.

(FRIDAY sits on ground. CRUSOE, cheerful, joins him.)

CRUSOE: Beautiful day again. Friday, I've decided to come fishing with you today. Just for fun.

FRIDAY: I cannot fish today.

CRUSOE: Why not? It's warm and the tides are right.

FRIDAY: The moon is wrong.

CRUSOE: Oh. How about a walk? Shoot a goat or two? Get a billy for dinner?

FRIDAY: No shooting today.

CRUSOE: What's wrong with today?

FRIDAY: You do not know Sorrow Day in England?

CRUSOE: Sorrow Day? Never heard of it.

FRIDAY: There are four times in the year when the moon is wrong. And those are the four days of sorrow.

CRUSOE: What are you supposed to do on Sorrow Day!

FRIDAY: You must sit upon the ground.

(CRUSOE squats beside FRIDAY.)

You must look at the ground. You must stare into the earth.

CRUSOE (trying this): How long for?

FRIDAY: All day long.

CRUSOE: And do nothing?

FRIDAY: You must do a great deal. You must stare into the earth until you see the faces.

CRUSOE: Whose faces?

FRIDAY: You will know them as soon as you see them. They will come to you.

CRUSOE: Whose faces?

FRIDAY: The faces of those you have lost.

CRUSOE: I can't see any faces in the earth.

FRIDAY: You must be patient. You must be quiet. You will see the faces.

(They both stare into the earth.)

CRUSOE: Still can't see any faces.

(No response from FRIDAY.)

Can you see faces?

(FRIDAY nods, after a pause.)

Who can you see?

FRIDAY: I can see children playing.

CRUSOE: But you have no children.

FRIDAY: My tribe has children.

CRUSOE: Friday, are you the father of some of those children?

FRIDAY: I may be. I may not be. It does not matter. They are the children of the tribe.

CRUSOE: But, Friday, that's terrible. You mean to tell me that you don't even —

FRIDAY: Quiet. I AM WATCHING THE CHILDREN.

CRUSOE: But —

FRIDAY: We do not talk on a Day of Sorrow. Stare into the earth. Have you lost nobody?

(CRUSOE is shocked. Then he realizes that he's hurt FRIDAY's feelings. FRIDAY and CRUSOE stare into the earth. Suddenly CRUSOE shuts his eyes and cries. FRIDAY, still staring into the earth, puts his hand on CRUSOE's shoulder to comfort him.)

DOCTOR: So he understood Sorrow Day?

FRIDAY (after a pause): Yes, he understood.

(Pause, then angrily, getting up.)

No, he understood nothing.

(CRUSOE puts on his gown and stands at the blackboard, his musket by his side instead of a stick. On the board he writes 'CIVILISATION'. FRIDAY sits for his lesson. CRUSOE stares at him in silence. FRIDAY smiles, CRUSOE stares.)

CRUSOE: Today you are not going to talk. There will be no questions today. There will be no singing. There will be no dancing.

(FRIDAY raises his hand.)

There will be no raising of hands. There will be no smiling. There will be no sighing. You understand?

(FRIDAY nods slowly three times.)

(Furious.) You don't understand. I will explain.

(He takes musket and begins to circle FRIDAY.)

I think you are very dangerous. I think, perhaps, you are an agent of the Devil. I have tried to show you what is good and what is bad. But you take the good things I show you and you twist them and you tear them apart until they lie bleeding. You take the bad things I show you and you smile as if they were your closest friends. But yesterday, with your Sorrow Day, you showed yourself most clearly. Yesterday you nearly enchanted me. For a time, for a time, I lost my soul.

(CRUSOE now stands quite still behind FRIDAY. FRIDAY raises his hand. His hand touches CRUSOE, who springs back and levels his musket.)

FRIDAY: I think you are beginning to sing, Master. But I do not think it is a true song.

(CRUSOE jams his rifle against FRIDAY's back.)

CRUSOE: Up on your feet.

(FRIDAY stands.)

Over to the board. Turn around.

(FRIDAY walks over to the blackboard and turns so that his back is to the board.)

Stay there.

(FRIDAY stands with his back to the board. CRUSOE goes into his corner. FRIDAY begins a solemn dance without moving from the spot.)

FRIDAY (sings to himself):
    There was a man whose skin was covered with thorns.
    There was a man whose skin was covered with thorns.
    There was a man whose skin was covered with thorns.

    May I take my knife and shave away your thorns?
    May I take my knife and shave away your thorns,
    So your skin may feel the fingers of the air?

(CRUSOE returns with the musket under one arm, chains over his shoulder. FRIDAY offers no resistance, but keeps singing while CRUSOE chains him to the blackboard.)

(Continues singing.)
    No, no, I am disarmed without my thorns,
    No, no, I am ashamed without my thorns.
    No, no, for your knife hurts my thorns so badly.

    There was a man whose skin was covered with thorns.
    There was a man whose skin was covered with thorns.
    There was a man —

(CRUSOE has now chained FRIDAY. He tears a lump from his black gown and stuffs it into FRIDAY's mouth. Then he takes another strip of gown and gags FRIDAY. CRUSOE stands back and stares at FRIDAY. CRUSOE advances on FRIDAY.)

CRUSOE (in cold anger): Today's lesson is about Man. Man. The earth belongs to Man. The animals belong to Man. So do the fish. And the birds. The trees. The grass. The stones. Man is the king of the earth. Under God.

Does this sound good? It is not good. Man is not good. But vile. A vile king. A scarlet monster in love with darkness. Because darkness hides him. And it is necessary for a monster to hide himself. Hide himself away. Yes.

But among those vile kings called men, there are some who can bear a little light. It hurts, but some of us can take the pain of that light. There are a few of us, only a few, to whom God has scattered a few grains of light. And we, my poor savage, are the leaders of men.

Yes. I'm one of those leaders. A king of kings, a vile king of vile kings. Why? Because I accept my vileness. I accept my scarlet monstrosity. I accept it all. I bow down to those more kingly than myself, more monstrous than me. And I make myself responsible for those who are less kingly, less monstrous.

I'm a vile king of vile kings because — because I use my will. Because, what I take, I keep. Because I have a gun. Because I have a pipe, I have rum, I have a hammock, razors, a grindstone, an axe, three Bibles, ink and paper, two barrels of gunpowder, a pair of scissors, books of navigation, three Bibles, a hammock . . . mathematical instruments, crowbars, canvas, pistols, planks of wood, compasses . . .

Because I do not flaunt my body because I know it is scarlet and monstrous. Because I am ashamed. Because I am proud to be ashamed. Because money is the fruit. No. I don't mean money. Yes. Because money is the root. Because I am rooted in money and shame because I am the vile king of the vile earth because I came to save you from your monstrosity by showing you how dark you are and how monstrous. Because I am scarlet and monstrously white. Because I am — because I have a gun.

(CRUSOE turns and walks away. FRIDAY is left chained and gagged. YOUNG MAN and GIRL run and free him.)

FRIDAY: That was my last lesson. After that I gave up trying to teach him. I worked, he gave me coins, I worked, he gave me coins, week after week, month after month . . .

(CRUSOE sits outside stockade, reading Bible. FRIDAY approaches dragging a heavy sack.)

CRUSOE: What've you got in there? Couple of goats?

FRIDAY: I've got a surprise for you.

(CRUSOE stands and walks over. FRIDAY lets sack fall. Many coins pour out. CRUSOE starts to pick them up, putting them back in the sack. FRIDAY climbs over the stockade ladder into the stockade. On ladder.)

Better count it all.

CRUSOE: You think I've got nothing better to do than count your money.

FRIDAY (from inside stockade): Not my money. Your money now.

CRUSOE: I don't need money. What use is money?

(FRIDAY's head reappears at top of stockade.)

FRIDAY: You're a rich man, Master. There are two thousand coins there. Count them.

CRUSOE: What are they for?

FRIDAY: You remember, we decided. The hut and everything in it. Two thousand. I shall sleep in the inner room. You may sleep in the stockade. And guard me.

CRUSOE: But there have to be two parties to a bargain. And I'm not selling. You can't make me sell.

(CRUSOE rushes to the ladder.)

FRIDAY: Surely you remember our agreement. Two thousand. The hut and everything in it. And look what I found in the hut.

(As CRUSOE reaches the base of the ladder, FRIDAY swings the gun-stick over the stockade and points it at CRUSOE. CRUSOE back away.)

CRUSOE: Now, Friday, don't do anything foolish. I've treated you like my own son. I've given you everything. When we first met, you were nothing but a savage. And I've educated you.

FRIDAY: When I first met you you were possessed by demons. Your head was full of nothing but your own power and your own guilt and the fear of a cruel God. And I taught you to dance, not very well, but I taught you that much at least. But perhaps I was a bad teacher. Because your head is still full of thoughts of power and guilt and fear.

CRUSOE: What are you going to do to me?

FRIDAY: I am going to make you work. You are going to work all day long. Instead of playing at work, you will work on that raft with all your strength, all day and every day. And I will stand over you with this gun while you work. And when the raft is finished, we will sail to Friday's island.

(CRUSOE goes outside. FRIDAY has finished his story. He takes off his drum and sits.)

DOCTOR: And so he worked, under the gun. And so you made him sail you back. And so you are home. And he waits outside. And he has asked to be admitted to the tribe.

(Some laughter, much chatter.)

No, he is serious. This Master wants to join the tribe. That is why the story is important.

YOUNG GIRL: He would corrupt the tribe. He is too full of fear.

YOUNG MAN: He might learn. We might learn from him. He has never lived in a tribe like ours. I think we should take him in.

YOUNG GIRL: He might betray us. He might have us all put in chains.

YOUNG MAN: But I think we should take him in. I think the tribe should share its love with him.

DOCTOR: He killed three of our good men.

YOUNG MAN: But he thought that they would kill him. And that was a long time ago.

DOCTOR: We will let him speak to us.

(YOUNG MAN goes to the door. TRIBE whisper. YOUNG MAN comes back in, followed by CRUSOE. CRUSOE takes off his hat, comes in humbly. Silence.)

CRUSOE: I don't know how to put this, but I would very much like to stay. I know that I've wronged your tribe in the past, when I shot those men, but it was simply that I didn't understand, and I know that I've often treated Friday here more harshly than he deserved, but I was only trying to help him develop as a —

(Smiles.)

civilized being. And if you'd let me join you, well I do have a number of skills which I could put at your disposal and I could teach you many things about that world outside and I could help to educate your children, —

(FRIDAY stands up.)

FRIDAY: It is not for me to decide. It is for the whole tribe. But I will say this — that I pity him because he is sick beyond the reach of all our magic. And I think he would destroy our tribe like a great sickness.

YOUNG GIRL: He killed two of our brothers.

YOUNG MAN: He had been taught to kill. If he can be taught to kill, he can be taught not to kill.

(Discussion on CRUSOE ad lib. FRIDAY playing no part. DOCTOR interested in CRUSOE's sickness. YOUNG GIRL strongly against his admission. YOUNG MAN undecided, wavering. Finally.)

DOCTOR: If he has a sickness of the mind, we can —

FRIDAY (turning round to audience): He has no sickness. He is sickness itself. He is a plague. And did you hear what this plague wants to do? He wants to teach our children. This plague wants our children.

CRUSOE: Well I only wanted to help you. But if you like I'll promise not to speak to the children.

FRIDAY: And now the plague makes promises. But who will guard him? Who will stand between the plague and our children? How can he join the tribe without talking with the children? Without its children the tribe does not exist? But let the tribe decide.

DOCTOR (to TRIBE and audience): Should we keep him? Keep him and try to teach him? Should we let him enter the tribe but keep him away from our children? Or should we send him back to the island he calls Mine?

(The audience decides. If CRUSOE expelled, he goes out. If admitted, he sits in corner quietly, head bowed, grateful, ashamed.)

TRIBE (sing):
> The Tribe changes
> As a tree changes.

FRIDAY (sings):
> When the storm throws its weight against a tree
> The tree bends away.
> When the storm falls asleep upon the tree
> The tree stands up again.

TRIBE (sing):
> The tribe changes
> As a tree changes.

FRIDAY (sings):
> The children are the blossoms of the tree.
> They laugh along the branches.
> The old are the fruit of the tree.
> They fall when they are ready to fall.

TRIBE (sing):
> The tribe changes
> As a tree changes.

FRIDAY (sings):
> Nobody tells the tree how it should grow.
> Nobody knows what shape it will assume.
> The tree decides angle of its branches.
> The tree decides when it is ready to die.

(During this song the TRIBE make a tree. They stand the tree on the ground and play their instruments, dancing at the same time. Everyone can dance.)

**The end**

# AS WE HAVE ALWAYS BEEN TOGETHER

*Gently, over sustained drone feeling (no beat)*

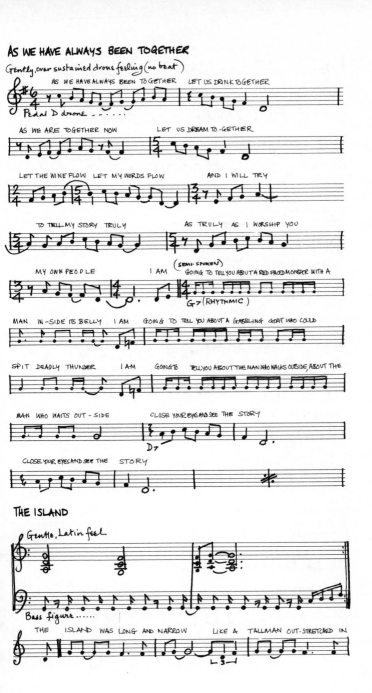

AS WE HAVE ALWAYS BEEN TOGETHER    LET US DRINK TOGETHER

*Pedal D drone - - - - - -*

AS WE ARE TOGETHER NOW        LET US DREAM TO-GETHER

LET THE WINE FLOW  LET MY WORDS FLOW        AND I WILL TRY

TO TELL MY STORY  TRULY           AS TRULY  AS  I WORSHIP YOU

MY OWN PEOPLE            I AM  (SEMI-SPOKEN) GOING TO TELL YOU ABOUT A RED FACED MONSTER WITH A

G7 (RHYTHMIC)

MAN  IN-SIDE ITS BELLY   I AM  GOING TO TELL YOU ABOUT A GABBLING GOAT WHO COULD

SPIT  DEADLY  THUNDER      I AM      GOING TO  TELL YOU ABOUT THE MAN WHO WALKS OUTSIDE  ABOUT THE

MAN  WHO WAITS OUT - SIDE      CLOSE YOUR EYES AND SEE THE  STORY

D7

CLOSE YOUR EYES AND SEE THE    STORY

# THE ISLAND

*Gentle, Latin feel*

*Bass figure......*

THE   ISLAND WAS LONG AND NARROW      LIKE A   TALL MAN  OUT-STRETCHED IN

# GOING TO RIDE (Raft Song)

ROCK FEEL  I  AM  GOING        TO RIDE            TO THE

A7

ISLAND        OF FRIDAY        ALL THE  TRIBE        WILL BE

A7                    D7              A7

WAITING        ON THE  BEACH        (OH  YEAH)          THERE'LL BE

D7                    A7                    D7

SINGING          AND      WEEPING    THERE'LL BE DANCING        AND

Bm7                      E7            Dm7

1.—LAUGHTER      THERE'LL BE   2.—LAUGHTER        I  AM  REPEAT FROM TOP

E7                        E7

# THERE WAS A MAN

Rock feel, bass doubles vocal line

Dm7

THERE WAS A MAN WHOSE SKIN WAS COVERED WITH THORNS

MAY I TAKE MY KNIFE AND SHAVE AWAY YOUR THORNS?
SO YOUR SKIN MAY FEEL THE FINGERS OF THE AIR?

NO NO I AM DISARMED WITHOUT MY THORNS
NO NO I AM ASHAMED WITHOUT MY THORNS
NO NO FOR YOUR KNIFE HURTS MY THORNS SO BADLY

THERE WAS A MAN WHOSE SKIN WAS COVERED WITH THORNS

# MIND YOUR HEAD

## Introduction

*Mind Your Head* is a show rather than a musical. It's more nearly related to panto than Broadway. If you want an image for the form, which is also the form of *Tyger*, my celebration of William Blake — think of a patchwork quilt. A patchwork quilt being waved vigorously like a flag. Some of the squares are dark, some are cheerful. They're sewn together with two of our best-known legends, Hamlet and Hitler.

Some clues to producing the show. However bizarre the behaviour of those around them, the characters should very rarely demonstrate any surprise. Many of the characters are cartoons, but not all of them. Character acting is essential, they should all take themselves very seriously. Laughs come from character and situation rather than from gags.

The play proper ends with the escape of Charlie Webb. With the appearance of Father Xmas the anti-masque begins and the pace should be break-neck — apart from the Conductress's singing of 'Calon Lan' and the delirious death speech of the Inspector.

The audience is asked to make quick changes of gear between the comic and the tragic, the satirical and the tender. But they are not asked for rounds after numbers and applause on exits.

Another image for the show — a truthful colour supplement. As you turn the pages, conflicting images hit you — a TV personality, a napalmed girl, a collector with his collection, a ballerina, Hitler, a rock singer. There is no overall message — see the song at the end of Act One.

*Mind Your Head* was commissioned by the Everyman Theatre, Liverpool, with the help of a grant from the Merseyside Arts Association. It was first performed at the Everyman Theatre on June 12th, 1973, with the following cast:

| | |
|---|---|
| VIKING | |
| BISCUITS BEIDERBECKE — A cheerful old man | |
| LORD BASIE — A gourmet | Richard Williams |
| SIR STANDARD THELONIUS — Jamaican businessman | |
| FREAK | |
| CHARLIE WEBB — A revolutionary | Jeffrey Kissoon |
| PEANUTS FITZGERALD — A civil servant | |
| BUMBO GILLESPIE — A TV personality | |
| LORD ELLINGTON — A golfer | Phillip Joseph |
| SEPTEMBER YARDBIRD — A ballerina | |
| MAHALIA SMITH | |
| LITTLE RED SCHOOLGIRL | |

| QUEEN ELIZABETH II<br>SOLDIER'S MOTHER | Angela Phillips |
|---|---|
| MISS ROVER<br>HOLLY TEAGARDEN – A housewife | Jean Hastings |
| MRS FITZGERALD<br>JELLYROLL HOLIDAY – A prostitute<br>THE POLKA-DOT NUN<br>ANGEL | Linda Beckett |
| DRIVER – Owen Stubber Junior | Jonathan Pryce |
| CONDUCTRESS – Myfanwy Stubber, mother of<br>    Owen Stubber Junior | Celia Hewitt |
| INSPECTOR – Claud Stubber, married to<br>    Myfanwy Stubber<br>GLUEPOT OLIVER – An extremely stupid person | Anthony Sher |
| THE GHOST OF OWEN STUBBER SENIOR<br>SOLDIER<br>CONDON MELLY – A drunk | Bernard Hill |
| CHUM RAINEY – A collector<br>HORACE HAMPTON – An impresario<br>MAN KENTON – Insurance Salesman<br>FARMER<br>CLERK<br>FATHER XMAS | Robert Putt |
| MUSICIANS | Anthony Haynes<br>John Fiske<br>Mike Innes<br>Tony Beaver |

REGAL PANTO HORSE
VULGAR PANTO STALLION
POLICEMEN AND POLICEWOMEN

Music by Antony Haynes
Directed by Alan Dossor

The London première of *Mind Your Head* was given by the Dolphin Theatre at the Shaw Theatre on January 30th 1974 with the following cast:

Barrie Rutter, Norman Beaton, David Casey, Lynda Marchal, June Watson, Lesley Joseph, Nicky Henson, Celia Hewitt, Ian Taylor, Sam Kelly, Robert Putt, Andy Roberts, David Richards, Robert Kirby, Ray Wehrstein.

Music by Andy Roberts
Directed by Peter James
Designed by Peter Ling

Special thanks are due to Alan Dossor who made many valuable suggestions about the text of *Mind Your Head.*

# Songs

**ACT ONE**

1 Overture. MUSICIANS
2 Heaven is a Hill called Hampstead — DRIVER and OTHERS
3 The Son of a Bitch — THELONIUS and OTHERS
4 Route 24. — DRIVER
5 Wash your Hands — FITZGERALD and MRS FITZGERALD
6 Here I comes — CHUM RAINEY
7 A Spell to Make a Bad Time Pass — FREAK
8 Oh That Tub! — BISCUITS BEIDERBECKE
9 Ball Game Song — MAHALIA SMITH
10 The Worst Thing in the World — DRIVER


**ACT TWO**

1 The Little Red Schoolgirl — THE LITTLE RED SCHOOLGIRL
2 Every Home Should Have One — FREAK
3 The Polka-Dot Coconut Man — THE POLKA-DOT NUN
4 The Marie Lloyd Song — DRIVER and CONDUCTRESS
5 Bad Friday — SOLDIER, FARMER, CLERK, ANGEL, SOLDIER'S MOTHER and OTHERS
6 The Revolution Never Stops — CHARLIE WEBB
7 Every Day is Christmas — FATHER XMAS
9 Marry Your Mother — FATHER XMAS and COMPANY
9 Calon Lan — CONDUCTRESS
10 Calon Lan and The Marie Lloyd Song — COMPANY

# ACT ONE

The stage is occupied by a red London double-decker bus.

This presents design and sight-line problems. Designer Peter Ling and his team solved these at Liverpool in the following way. Presented with an old double-decker bus by the Merseyside Passenger Transport Authority, they cut it into sections. On stage they placed the driver's cab so that it faced the audience. The passenger section – with one wall cut away, ran straight across the back of the stage. The rear section of the bus was placed at an angle – so that the bus looked as if it were going round two almost right-angle bends. Ceilings were welded in curves so that it didn't look like an articulated vehicle. Lights and bells worked and great care was taken with details – like obtaining exactly the right shades of paint for the ceilings and exterior of the bus. The bus they made was a beautiful combination of realism and fantasy.

The route number of the bus is 24. The front roller says:

>24  CAMDEN TOWN
>HAMPSTEAD ROAD
>CHARING CROSS ROAD
>WHITEHALL  VICTORIA
>PIMLICO

Above the DRIVER's cab is a sign saying THE RED REVENGER.

On one side of the roller is an advert saying YES.

On the other side is an advert saying NO.

The rear adverts on the bus say SOONER and OR LATER.

There is also a detachable advert for 'Daddie's Favourite Sauce' in the bus.

There is a bin for used tickets marked USED TICKETS. A sign says: 72 PASSENGERS – 32 LOWER DECK 40 UPPER DECK. There is a luggage alcove under the stairs.

Instruments are set out for the musicians in the lower saloon. Seats can be movable – old tram seats which have movable backs so that the passengers can face either way are recommended. A way should be found to suggest when the bus is moving and when it is at rest. In the DRIVER's cab and on the platform of the bus there are microphones – so the DRIVER can make bus engine noises and brake noises.

There must be an acting area in front of the bus.

About ten minutes before the show starts, a VIKING warrior walks on to the forestage with a DOG. VIKING is heavily armed with dagger, sword, spear, shield, horned helmet, flowing blonde wig and spectacles. He is tentative but friendly. He faces the audience rather than the bus, with occasional glances to make sure that the bus hasn't been nicked. Sometimes he consults an hourglass which is strapped to his wrist. The DOG is any equable dog, but not a guard dog. Now and then VIKING tells the audience 'It'll start in about eight minutes', 'Five minutes to go' and so on. More often he will appear to be about to speak and decide not to. Sometimes he squats and mutters to his DOG.

Bedraggled MUSICIANS enter one by one and slump into their places. Other passengers follow. If a curtain in front of the bus is feasible, they should queue at a bus stop in front of curtains.

MISS ROVER, a lonely, middle-aged, working-class woman in her best clothes, who is given to reading out signs and advertisements and street names aloud, plods on to the bus and sits in a front seat on the upper deck.

PEANUTS FITZGERALD is next aboard — a smooth-mannered middle-aged man with an umbrella and the air of a civil servant who is used to giving commands. He takes a seat on the lower deck.

Next SIR STANDARD THELONIUS, a black and very prosperous Jamaican businessman takes another seat on the lower deck.

SEPTEMBER YARDBIRD, a ballerina in a tutu, pirouettes on to the forestage, peers around for the bus in ballet style, does a leap on to the platform, dances gracefully up the stairs and into a back seat in the upper saloon.

THELONIUS reads *The Times*, PEANUTS reads the *Telegraph*, MISS ROVER observes the view and YARDBIRD chews bubble gum and blows bubbles.

VIKING (thumping spear on stage three times): Munuc hatte Abbo!
Evening all! The overture!

(MUSICIANS remain asleep.)

Sorry folks, slight delay. You see the band's been up all night playing at the Neo-Marxist Embroidery and Valeta Championship in Hampstead.

(To MUSICIANS.)

We're waiting, gentlemen.

(MUSICIANS stir.)

And, er, they're on this buzz, this 24 London buzz, which is parked at South End Green, Hampstead, London. And the buzz will be ready to take them all the way home to Pimlico as soon as they've given us

(Shouts.)

THE OVERTURE!

(MUSICIANS respond, get ready.)

(Shaking head.)

Artists, artists!

(MUSICIANS shake their heads.)

Well, here comes the music so — MIND YOUR HEAD!

(MUSICIANS gallop through the overture while the VIKING makes tentative Hooray Harry Movements. At the end, VIKING applauds mildly.)

That was terrible.

MISS ROVER (to herself as she surveys South End Green. Looking ahead): Fancy having two traffic islands. Two islands. Both got benches and old men on them. Well, this island, just down here, it's got a Gents and Ladies and a green shelter for the busmen. But that one over there, it's got two patches of grass and a monument. I like the island with the monument better. The old men on the benches on that island look nicer than the old men on the benches on this island.

VIKING: The road here is cobbled with cube-shaped cobbles, coloured slate blue, brick-red and grey. These could be levered up easily for use as missiles in case of an insurrection. But no insurrection is expected.

(DRIVER enters in a good mood. He wears driver's uniform, a mourning band and carries a snap tin. He is OWEN STUBBER JUNIOR, a Welsh cockney.)

DRIVER: They've given me a new bus. They say its nifty round corners.

(Sees bus.)

Jesus Christ on toast, that's a novelty.

(He inspects the bus.)

VIKING (producing newspaper): I've got another surprise for the driver. *News of the World* reporters have been investigating the astonishing nocturnal activities of the Goosers. They are a sect of groupie girls addicted to buses and bus drivers. Who are they? Why do they look to bus drivers for their kicks?

DRIVER: She's eccentric, capricious, colourful, buxom, responsive, original and beautiful. It's love at first sight. Thank you very much.

VIKING: Now listen to this Owen. 'Sirens of the Buses. The late night Liverpool bus stopped. All the passengers got off, all except for a girl. Within seconds the girl was locked in a passionate embrace with the driver.'

DRIVER: A likely story.

(VIKING hands him the paper.)

VIKING: 'Unlikely? Don't you believe it. *News of the World* reporters found the goosers.'

DRIVER (continues): 'At the end of a bus ride, many of these girls expect to go all the way with the driver. The nicknames conjured up for the goosers by busmen are far from complimentary: Dogface, The Muirhead Bike and the Pouncer. At Liverpool's Pier Head Depot we talked to a driver's mate named Buckminster Smith and asked how he came to be nicknamed "Oliver". Said Buckie:'

VIKING (Liverpool accent): ' "There was a crowd of us in the pub having a game of darts when a gooser came in. The boys bought her a few drinks and in the conversation that followed a challenge was made and accepted." '

DRIVER (dreamily): A challenge was made and accepted.

VIKING (Liverpool accent): ' "We went over the road and used the end bus. I can even remember the number – 169. I went back to the pub, had another three pints and then went back to the gooser on the bus. That's why they call me Oliver – the one who went back for more."

DRIVER: Why do they do it?

VIKING: ' "The uniform plays some part in it, I think," said an auburn-haired girl who left school last year.

DRIVER: 'She said that she was known to the busmen as the "Netherley Nymph" ' – the Netherley Nymph – oh God –

(Rushes to the platform, shouts up the stairs.)

Any goosers, any goosers up there?

CONDUCTRESS (she is also cockney-Welsh, MYFANWY STUBBER, OWEN's mother. She wears uniform, plus a bridal veil and confetti. To audience): The air looks all grainy, like wood.

(Coughs.)

DRIVER: Hello Mother.

CONDUCTRESS: I can't remember drinking but I must have been drinking. Everything tastes like liver this morning. Owen! Haven't you noticed anything?

DRIVER: Yes, we've got one of those new open plan buses.

VIKING: You have indeed. It's the new Norwegian Red Revenger, manufactured by the Ibsen Omnibus Company.

CONDUCTRESS: Owen. I'm not only your conductress, I'm your mother. Look at me.

(Takes off veil. DRIVER looks, walks over, brushes off confetti.)

DRIVER: You've caught some kind of technicolour dandruff.

CONDUCTRESS (stepping dramatically on to platform): I got married. Again.

VIKING: The swept turning cycle is seventy-one feet.

(DRIVER, outraged, runs to mother and thrusts out and taps the mourning band on his arm.)

DRIVER: You're not meant to be marrying, you're meant to be mourning. Dad only shuffled off his mortal a month ago.

CONDUCTRESS: Thirty-one lonely days and nights.

VIKING: Air suspension is provided fore and after. There is ample provision for the accommodation of a musical group in the lower saloon.

(DRIVER rushes back to cab, grabs snap tin, back to platform, opens tin, produces skull.)

DRIVER (to skull): There she is Dad, in all her gory glory. What about it Dad? Are you going to bless the bride?

CONDUCTRESS: I've got a hangover. I feel like the Hanging Gardens of
   Babylon.

DRIVER: And who's the lucky maniac? Some male gooser? The Pimlico
   Puller?

VIKING: The whole vehicle has the height of a normal low-bridge double-
   decker with, paradoxically, an orthodox highbridge seating arrangement —

DRIVER: Whom have you married, mother. Whom? Whom? Whom?

CONDUCTRESS: Your own dear father's brother. Your jovial uncle —

DRIVER: Claud?

CONDUCTRESS: Claud.

DRIVER: *Claud.*

   (Addresses audience.)

   My name is Owen Stubber. I live two doors away from my mother
   Myfanwy in the cockney-Welsh ghetto of Kilburn. I'm a driver on the
   number 24 route from South End Green, Hampstead, to Pimlico and
   back again. And round and round you know. And so was

   (Putting his cap on the skull.)

   my late father before me. And the Inspector on this route is my clammy
   Uncle Claud. Yuck. Another busman, but no more like my father than
   Stirling Moss to the late Sir Gerald Nabarro.

CONDUCTRESS: Claud's an Inspector. Claud's a born leader.

DRIVER: I hate born leaders. Oh why, mother? Why?

CONDUCTRESS: The uniform plays some part in it, I think.

DRIVER: I am seized up with psychic agony, but if I must be seized up
   with psychic agony, I would rather be seized up with psychic agony in the
   postal district of North West Three than anywhere else on earth —
   because . . .

DRIVER AND OTHERS (sing):
   Heaven is a hill called Hampstead.
   And Hampstead is heaven on a hill.

   There's the garden where Keats heard the nightingale.
   There's a scruffy little pub where they still serve ale.
   There's a marvellous choice of secondary schools —
   Some for the rich and some for the fools.

   Heaven is a hill called Hampstead
   And Hampstead is heaven on a hill.

   Twice a year on the Heath they hold a wonderful fair.
   You can see the working classes there.
   Eighty thousand for a cottage but nobody cares
   In a street of socialist millionaires.

Heaven is a hill called Hampstead
And Hampstead is heaven on a hill.

Daddy's drinking champers on an ocean liner
On his way to study acupuncture in China.
Did you ever hear a German girl swear?
Mummy wrote a novel about the au pair.

Heaven is a hill called Hampstead.
And Hampstead is heaven on a hill —

Yes we'll take our stand
In liberal land,
Home of the financially free,
In heaven, heaven,
Heavenly, heavenly
Hampstead North West Three.

DRIVER: My heart may be breaking — but the number 24 has got to go through.

VIKING: I hope you like the way we've incorporated a squarer radiator grill . . .

CONDUCTRESS: Mind your head!

(Exit VIKING. Bus starts. Passengers rise, bump their heads. CONDUCTRESS picks up microphone by luggage compartment.)

CONDUCTRESS: Good morning. I am Myfanwy Stubber, your omnibus hostess. May I welcome you on board on behalf of London Transport. In the unlikely event of an emergency you will observe that there are dirty old copies of *The Sun* underneath your seats . . .

DRIVER (into fixed mike): Hello, this is your driver, Owen Stubber Junior. We're now about 200 feet above sea-level, visibility is groggy, we expect to average a good 14 miles per hour and we should reach our destination Pimlico in about 45 minutes from now. Have a pleasant trip . . .

MISS ROVER: Constantine Road — I like One Way Streets. Bombay Restaurant.

(CONDUCTRESS enters lower saloon.)

CONDUCTRESS: Fares please.

FITZGERALD (offering ten p): Ten p and keep the change, Miss.

CONDUCTRESS: Mrs. Mrs Mrs, in fact. Twice married.

FITZGERALD: The uniform plays some part in it, I think.

CONDUCTRESS: No, it's more likely the breasts. They're quite large.

MISS ROVER: Agincourt Road. Agincourt was a battle. We won. I saw that film.

FITZGERALD: Your breasts are your own concern — shall we concentrate on the business in hand? I've got ten p, you've got a ten p ticket. Is it a deal?

CONDUCTRESS: Are you a bloody Tory?

FITZGERALD: That's my business.

CONDUCTRESS: Only a bloody Tory says: that's my business. Double fare, comrade. Twenty p.

MISS ROVER: And there's Cressy Road. We won that battle too. I don't think there was a film though.

FITZGERALD: Shall we make it fifteen p?

CONDUCTRESS: Don't try your laissez-faire on me. This is a socialist bus. Pay up — twenty.

FITZGERALD: I'd like to make one thing perfectly clear —

CONDUCTRESS (grabbing him by the lapels): Only five people are allowed to stand on the lower deck. Unless you can find four others to stand with you, you'd better sit down.

(CONDUCTRESS pushes him down.)

FITZGERALD (sitting): I'd simply say this —

CONDUCTRESS: And no spitting. Pay up.

FITZGERALD (paying): Under protest.

CONDUCTRESS: Granted.

(CONDUCTRESS zips off tickets for and takes fares from MUSICIANS. Then she approaches THELONIUS.)

CONDUCTRESS: Bloodytory?

THELONIUS (proferring ten pound note): One first class single to Malden Road, if you'd be so good.

CONDUCTRESS: What's that? Ten pound note? We're not obliged to take tenners.

THELONIUS: Keep the change for your bottom drawer.

CONDUCTRESS: Very thoughtful.

(Gives him ticket, pockets note.)

You're not a retired busman are you?

THELONIUS: Hardly, madam.

(Gives her a visiting card.)

CONDUCTRESS (reads it): Sir Standard Thelonius. Multi-Millionaire.

DRIVER, CONDUCTRESS, MUSICIANS, MISS ROVER, FITZGERALD and YARDBIRD (sing, in an envious mutter):
    The son of a bitch
    Is as rich as rich
    Can be.

I wish we could switch
So the son of a bitch
Was me.
But however much I envy him for what
                      he's got
However much I hate his guts for what
                      I'm not
He don't care.

THELONIUS (sings):
I don't care.

OTHERS (sing):
He don't care.

THELONIUS (sings):
I don't care.
Cos I'm a guaranteed twenty-four carat
                      tycoon
With a gold-plated swivel chair.
I'm mister ten thousand and eighty per cent —
The self-made millionaire.

OTHERS (sing in dying fall):
The son of a bitch
Is as rich as rich
Can be.
I wish we could switch
So the son of a bitch
Was me.

THELONIUS: I'm the director of a group of West Indian companies. We're moving into the British market rather heavily.

MISS ROVER: Southampton Road. Yanks out of Vietnam. Have a happy old age, says Dame Sybil Thorndike.

THELONIUS: I've already taken over White Horse Whisky, Lever Brothers, Shell United Dairies and Barclays Bank. Moving our lads into top executive positions, you know.

CONDUCTRESS: What about our lads?

THELONIUS: We've made a bulk purchase of the Yorkshire Dales National Park. It'll be converted into a cabbage plantation. Oh there'll be plenty of jobs for English cabbage-pluckers.

CONDUCTRESS: What if the English won't stand for that?

THELONIUS: Up to them. They can compose beautiful spirituals about the trouble they're seeing — or they can ask their overseer for a transfer to a chain gang in Surrey.

CONDUCTRESS: But don't you think you're asking for a little massacre? Coming over here, buying up our lovely industries, setting up a slavery system based on chains and nobody knows the cabbage I seen? Where's your awareness of your own racial history?

THELONIUS: A businessman is a businessman. I'm not black. I'm not white. I'm just rich.

CONDUCTRESS: Look, if you're the Howard Hughes of the Caribbean, where's your Cadillac?

THELONIUS: Outside the Dorchester. I'm gaining first-hand experience of bus travel because I'm considering a take-over bid. Your government is hiving off London Transport to private enterprise. And that's me.

CONDUCTRESS: You'll never make a profit out of buses. White elephants, they are.

THELONIUS: Not after we've rationalized the system by introducing our own remuneration structure over here.

CONDUCTRESS: You mean we'll be put on West Indian wages?

(Clumping upstairs.)

Hey, you just wait for the Revolution, mate.

THELONIUS: I'm waiting, lady.

(Exit from bus platform as if bus still moving.)

MISS ROVER: Women Live! What does that mean?

(CONDUCTRESS thumps up the stairs.)

CONDUCTRESS: Fares please!

MISS ROVER: I'm a Red Rover.

(Shows ticket, looks out of window.)

The Gypsy Queen, romantic-looking pub. That's a good name for a barber's shop — Keep Your Hair On.

CONDUCTRESS (to YARDBIRD): Bloodytory?

YARDBIRD (rising and dancing as she speaks, dancing all through the ensuing speech, down the stairs and along the lower saloon, followed by clumping CONDUCTRESS): I'm a political anomaly. I'm a defecting ballerina. And my name's September Yardbird and it doesn't sound Russian because I'm not Russian and you haven't heard of me because nobody writes about me and they don't write about me because I'm not very good. That's why I'm defecting to Russia. I shall go to the Bolshoi and tell them the story of how I was oppressed by Covent Garden who only let me dance in decadent, jazz-corrupted works.

MISS ROVER: Neighbourhood Advice Centre. Maria Simpson is mad and she knows it.

(DRIVER stops bus, comes round the platform.)

YARDBIRD: And I shall be the toast of Leningrad and Moscow, and I shall spend my weekends writing a book all about my miserable life in Russia and when I'm touring in Britain or Australia I'll defect to the West as a prima ballerina and the *Sunday Times* will serialize my story. And I shall make a Nobel prize speech in which I shall denounce the Nobel Prize.

DRIVER: This bus has no licence for dancing.

YARDBIRD: Then we'd better sing. I feel like singing. It's a beautiful bus.

DRIVER: Unique I'd call it.

YARDBIRD: And you drive it magnificently.

DRIVER: You're not the Netherley Nymph, are you?

CONDUCTRESS: No, she's a defective ballerina.

YARDBIRD: I *do* love this route.

DRIVER: Now you're talking.

(Sings.)

> If you really want to move it, come along with us
> For a double-decker daydream on a London bus.
> Well the number of the bus is 24
> And the route's so cool that you'll scream for more.

MUSICIANS:
> Where does it go?

DRIVER:
> Pimlico

MUSICIANS:
> Where has it been?

DRIVER:
> South End Green.

MUSICIANS:
> Give us a break
> What route does it take?

DRIVER:
> Well you've been so great
> That I'll elucidate —
> South End Green is where it starts of course
> Then it turns sharp left at the Old White Horse
> Past St Dominic's Church and The Gipsy Queen
> Now we've really taken off from South End Green.

MUSICIANS:
> 24
> Give us some more

DRIVER:
> Malden Road and Malden Crescent
> Ferdinand Street where the chips are pleasant

Chalk Farm Road for a second-hand bed
Then bang into Hawley Street and past The Nag's Head.

Kentish Town
Camden Road and Bayham
Non Ferrous Founders — Precision Engineers
Crowndale Road
Hurdwick Place and Hampstead
Then The Royal Ear Hospital for royal ears.

MUSICIANS:

Please Mister 24.
Give us just a little more.

DRIVER:

Gower Street
Bloomsbury
Shaftesbury Avenue
Charing Cross Road
And now
Nelson's in view
Veer round The Square
Down Whitehall
Parliament Square
Is our next call.

Westminster Abbey
Victoria Street
And an office where
Unemployed draughtsmen meet
Past British Rail
At Victoria Station
Tender your fare
And state your destination
Vauxhall Bridge Road
Neathouse Place
Then the river and the
Power station
Stare you in the face.

Pimlico!
That's the way we go

When we travel by the river
I give a hoot
And then it's back to Hampstead

MUSICIANS:

Then it's back to Hampstead

DRIVER:

With minor variations

MUSICIANS:
    Minor variations
DRIVER:
    On the southbound
    Famous
    Swinging
    Number 24 route!

MISS ROVER: There seems to be a lot of singing on buses these days. I hope they've got permission from someone.

(YARDBIRD exits. DRIVER goes back to his cab. In his seat is the GHOST OF THE DRIVER'S FATHER, in ghastly grey-green busman's uniform. DRIVER thinks he must have got the wrong bus, wheels away, then, not seeing his bus anywhere else around, goes back, checks number plate.)

DRIVER: Out you hop, chum. That's my chariot.

(GHOST slowly descends and approaches DRIVER, with arms outstretched.) DRIVER retreats. GHOST tries to embrace him. DRIVER wriggles away.)

(Backing towards cab.)

You can knock that off for a start. I'm not prejudiced, mind. It's just not my particular sexual territory.

(DRIVER climbs in cab.)

You must be on the number eleven route.

(To Audience.)

They're all as queer as diesel-driven whippets on the number elevens. Chelsea.

(GHOST stands in front of bus.)

Go on, sunshine, out of my way if you don't want to get merged with my underfloor-mounted engine-gearbox assembly.

(GHOST doesn't move. CONDUCTRESS rings bell twice.)

That's my mum ringing the bell. One for stop, two for go, three for what the bloody hell's going on?

(GHOST writhes in horror at mention of DRIVER's mother.)

(To Audience.)

Blimey, we've really got one here.

(DRIVER gets out of cab, limbers up like a boxer, goes and stands nose to nose with GHOST. GHOST reaches out for him, DRIVER dodges back.)

Right, what's your trouble?

(GHOST indicates that he can't talk.)

Hungry? Thirsty? I see, you're dumb. Well, I can't help you with that mate, but I could drop you off at the Clinical Pharmacology Medical Unit in Gower Street. Just by RADA.

(GHOST mimes 'no'.)

(Resigned, leaning on cab)

Go on then, do us a Marcel Marceau.

(GHOST thinks, then points to his eye. Ad libs are OK during this passage.)

Good. That's 'I'.

(GHOST gets down on all fours and roots like a pig.)

Anteater? I anteater? No?

(GHOST mimes curly tail.)

I Hoover? I pig?

(GHOST nods.)

I pig?

(GHOST shakes head, pretends to cut own throat.)

I dead pig?

(GHOST mimes 'Getting warmer'.)

Dead pig? I bacon? I ham?

(GHOST nods.)

I ham?

(GHOST nods, thinks, then pats thigh. Then slaps it.)

I am leg? No. I ham – are you all right? I ham thigh? I ham Oklahoma? I ham thigh?

(GHOST gives thumbs up then indicates 'Hold it'.)

OK, take your time.

(GHOST rushes into bus unnoticed by CONDUCTRESS and PASSENGERS. GHOST takes advertising placard which says 'Daddie's Favourite Sauce'. Rushes back to DRIVER, holds it up.)

I ham thigh Daddie's Favourite Sauce.

(GHOST angrily shakes head, covers up all but the first three letters of the placard.)

I ham thigh Dad. I am thy Dad. Hello, Dad, sorry, it's all that green stuff on you. I knew I remembered your face from somewhere . . .

(DRIVER passing radiator, puts hand on skull, suddenly realizes what he's got his hand on.)

Wait a minute – my Dad's dead.

(GHOST nods.)

Then you're a – go on, pull the other one it's got

(CONDUCTRESS rings bell three times.)

on. There's no such thing as — you're just some weird kind of joker looks a bit like my Dad and you're — never will understand blokes like you.

(CONDUCTRESS comes round to the front of the bus. GHOST recoils in horror.)

Don't go like that —

(Imitates recoil.)

— at my mother.

CONDUCTRESS (scrutinizing DRIVER): So you finally got there, did you?

DRIVER: Where?

CONDUCTRESS: Round the bloody twist. What's the hold-up? We've got to get going Owen.

DRIVER: How can we Myfanwy? It's this bloke here, you'll never believe it mum, but he was trying to scare me —

CONDUCTRESS: What bloke?

DRIVER: This — you mean nobody else can see you?

(DRIVER turns round but GHOST shakes head. DRIVER jumps in the air, walks round in small circles whistling tunelessly, then whooshes round into his cab. Exit GHOST.)

All right Mum, just one of me turns, be all right in a minute.

CONDUCTRESS (returning to platform): Better had be.

FITZGERALD: Is there something psychologically wrong with that driver?

CONDUCTRESS: He's all right basically. Just mind *your* head.

(FITZGERALD rises, hits head, sits. GHOST appears beside DRIVER's cab from engine if possible. DRIVER mimes: 'I surrender.')

DRIVER: Look Dad, you died a month ago, right? Drowned when you were bumped into the Thames by a black bus with no number plates. And they never found the driver.

(GHOST points out of cab to sign on front of bus. DRIVER cranes to read it.)

Red Revenger? You want revenge? Fair enough. But who did you, Dad?

(Enter INSPECTOR, CLAUD STUBBER. He wears black Inspector's uniform and bears a marked resemblance to Hitler, although his forelock is hidden by his cap. He stands in front of the bus. GHOST points accusingly at INSPECTOR.)

Claud! So it was Claud.

INSPECTOR (starting casually, but with hysteria mounting as he begins to enjoy having an audience): The responsibilities of an Inspector of buses are manifold. He must enforce the scheduled timetables. He must supervise the conduct of the crews, reprimanding laxity and reporting breaches of the regulations. He must scrutinize the buses on his route, checking their efficiency and smartness. He must cleanse the passenger areas of all such threats to public order as the seat-cover slasher, the defiler of advertisements and the Irish tenor. But, above all, the Inspector, by his own probity in power, must set an example to his underlings. And where, in this corrupted metropolis, will we find such a man?

CONDUCTRESS: Oh, there you are, Claud!

(GHOST urges DRIVER to driver on. DRIVER starts up.)

DRIVER (to GHOST): I can't just flatten him like that.

(GHOST makes threatening gesture. DRIVER shrugs and starts moving.)

CONDUCTRESS: Why are you standing in the middle of the road then?

INSPECTOR: Halt! I order you to halt!

(DRIVER brakes rapidly. Everyone jerks on bus.)

MISS ROVER: Tyre Safety Week. I never knew it was Tyre Safety Week.

INSPECTOR (approaching cab): You need prosecution, you Jehu.

DRIVER: What you call me, comrade?

INSPECTOR: Jehu. Second book of Kings, chapter nine, verse 18. 'The driving is like the driving of Jehu, the son of Nimshi; for he driveth furiously.' Bloody Jehu.

(CONDUCTRESS walks round and embraces INSPECTOR. GHOST rages.)

How is my bride this morning?

CONDUCTRESS: Oh God, Claud. My brain is half-submerged in a puddle of stale barley wine.

INSPECTOR (to DRIVER): Why do you stare? Have you never seen a loving couple before?

DRIVER: Yes. At the Essoldo, Kilburn. Belgian Busmen on the Job.

INSPECTOR: But tell me, nephew, are you sick or tired or stupid? You have parked your bus in Malden Road for ten minutes and then charged towards your Inspector like a berserk rhinoceros. Tonight you will be on report. I shall now inspect your interior.

(INSPECTOR and CONDUCTRESS walk back to platform, followed by GHOST. Before they can get on, DRIVER starts up. INSPECTOR and CONDUCTRESS have to run (on the spot) to catch up, jumping on at last minute. GHOST is left to do sideways walk off-stage to indicate being left behind, giving rude sign to INSPECTOR as he goes. INSPECTOR walks along lower saloon, stops beside FITZGERALD.)

All tickets!

FITZGERALD: Inspector, it's a funny thing, but you remind me of someone, name's on the tip of my tongue, don't tell me —

INSPECTOR (with sidelong glance): Oh yes, I'm always being mistaken for him. You mean —

(INSPECTOR takes bowler and cane and does Charlie Chaplin walk all around the forestage and back.)

We're related on my mother's side.

FITZGERALD: Nice. Inspector, I wish to make a complaint about your conductress. She has been adjusting our fares according to our political inclinations.

INSPECTOR: I ought to warn you about frivolous complaints, sir —

FITZGERALD: I am not frivolous.

INSPECTOR: Then what is your position in life?

(FITZGERALD walks to the platform, tendering his ticket. FITZGERALD'S WIFE appears towards side of stage.)

FITZGERALD (sings):
>My well-swept house is almost in the country
>You can see woodlands from the upstairs window
>On Saturday and Sunday there's a deck-chair on the patio
>And there I drink a can or two of lager.

FITZGERALD'S WIFE (sings):
>Oh wash your hands, my darling,
>Wash your hands, my darling,
>Wash your clever hands.

FITZGERALD (sings):
>With my arm across my eyelids, I sleep very soundly.
>My wife likes Chopin but I favour Mantovani
>My little girl of five goes to ballet class on Wednesday.
>My little boy of seven collects toy vehicles.

FITZGERALD'S WIFE (sings):
>Oh wash your hands, my darling,
>Wash your hands, my darling.
>Wash your gentle hands.

FITZGERALD (sings):
>Every other weekend I take to my mother
>A cake from the kitchen or flowers from the garden.
>I always have a word and wave for the neighbours
>As I go to do the work which I never mention.

FITZGERALD'S WIFE (sings):
>Oh wash your hands, my darling,
>Wash your hands, my darling,
>Wash your loving hands.

FITZGERALD (sings):

> Sometimes I sit and stare at nothing
> Sometimes I sit and smile at nothing
> Sometimes I sit and think of nothing
> My job is torturing men and women
> My job is torturing men and women
> My job is —

FITZGERALD'S WIFE (sings):

> Oh wash your hands, my darling
> Wash your hands, my darling,
> Wash your shaking hands.

(Exit MRS FITZGERALD.)

INSPECTOR: Well, somebody has to do it, sir.

FITZGERALD: Precisely. If I didn't, somebody else would. This is Chalk Farm Road, I believe?

(FITZGERALD begins to leave.)

INSPECTOR: Certainly, sir.

(FITZGERALD goes off-stage watched by MISS ROVER.)

MISS ROVER: That's funny . . . He's unlocking the door to a big office building. He's going in. But the whole building looks as if it's empty. It says Keep Out. It says Guard Dogs Loose On These Premises.

INSPECTOR: An impressive man.

(Getting off bus.)

I will see you later, Myfanwy. Keep an eye on that unstable son of yours.

(Exits.)

CONDUCTRESS: Bye bye my love. Mind your head.

DRIVER: Next time. I'll get him next time, Dad. I think.

MISS ROVER: Paddy's Autos. There's a nice pawnshop. Thirteen Murders in Derry. When was that? Oh they've got the Wrath of God on at the Plaza. Chalk Farm Road.

CONDUCTRESS (on top deck): Any more? Any more?

MISS ROVER: I'm the Red Rover.

CONDUCTRESS: Course you are dear, clean forgot.

MISS ROVER: Camden Road. Victory Hairdressing Saloon. J. Moss, Orthopaedic Mechanicians. Hampstead Road, Those tall flats have nice names — Dalehead, Gillfoot, Rydal Water, Cartmel. National Temperance Hospital. Unwanted goods Wanted.

CONDUCTRESS (rings bell, bus stops): Gower Street.

MISS ROVER: What a lot of hospitals. Comforting.

(A large man called CHUM RAINEY, wearing a bowler hat and spectacles, very genial, gets on bus. CHUM carries a bucket carefully. The bucket has a lid on it and the word BUMS painted on it. A SOLDIER, a private with rifle and kitbag, comes up to bus.)

CONDUCTRESS: Hurry along please.

SOLDIER: Shaftesbury Avenue?

CONDUCTRESS (as bus starts): Yes.

(SOLDIER jumps on bus.)

CHUM (giving way): Soldiers first, it's an old tradition on the 24 route.

(CHUM and SOLDIER sit down.)

You from London, squaddie?

SOLDIER: Yorkshire. London's a bloody dump.

CHUM: Don't worry, you'll see the world.

SOLDIER: It's a turd's life in the Army.

CHUM: Let me cheer you up. I'm good at it. I once read a very good book about cheering people up called 'How to Cheer People Up'. The first rule was: Get people to talk about themselves. What's your hobby?

SOLDIER: Haven't got one. Not any more.

CHUM: Well, what was your hobby?

SOLDIER: I used to go in for matchboxes. Captain Webb matchboxes. He was the first man to swim the Channel. British. He did it in 1875.

CHUM: Covered in grease, was he?

SOLDIER: I don't think so. He had a big moustache. And a striped bathing costume. Anyway, I collected about five thousand empty matchboxes with pictures of Captain Webb on them. And then I used them to make a model of the Taj Mahal in the garden.

CHUM: Impressive.

SOLDIER: No, it wasn't. I mean it were right shape for Taj Mahal. But real Taj Mahal isn't covered with thousands of portraits of Captain Webb, is it?

CHUM: Wouldn't know.

SOLDIER: It just stood there in the garden looking awful. Even by moonlight. Captain Webb's Taj Mahal.

CHUM: What happened to it?

SOLDIER: I tried to burn it down. But rain had made it soggy so I kicked it to bits. Useless. I'm pretty bloody useless most ways.

CHUM: Oh. Then talking about you won't cheer you up. Let's talk about me instead. I'm a collector too.

SOLDIER: What d'you collect?

(CHUM taps his bucket.)

B.U.M.S. What does that stand for?

CHUM: Bums. Yes, bums.

SOLDIER: What've you got in it?

CHUM: Couple of bums.

SOLDIER: You don't mean — human bums?

CHUM: Oh yes, human bums. Off people. Bums in alcohol. Keeps them fresh. Just picked up a brace of them from the hospital. I've got a friend who's a surgeon. Slips me the odd bum half price.

SOLDIER: So you're one of them bum collectors?

CHUM: Right first time. Keep 'em in storage jars, all classified and catalogued. Serious collector. I don't play with them or anything. There are hundreds of us you know. Oh yes, I correspond with bum collectors all over the world. That's mainly because I run a magazine, you may have seen it in Smith's — *The Bum Collector.* Here, take a copy.

(Gives SOLDIER magazine.)

SOLDIER: You're cheering me up already. Any particular type of bums you collect? Specially big bums or something?

CHUM: No, no, just famous bums. Got some good ones.

SOLDIER: Whose bums would you most like to collect?

CHUM: Of course my ambition has always been Brigitte Bardot. But Billy Bremner would be something of a prize.

SOLDIER: Max Bygraves?

CHUM: No, I wouldn't give you a Robin Day for that. Trouble is, of course, most of the best bums tend to go to the States. Yes, there's quite a bum drain. Edward Heath's bum is in the University of Texas. Shameful really. Still, I stay pretty cheerful. And as I stroll around London on my bum-spotting jaunts, I often sing this little song :

(CHUM walks to the platform and on to forestage.)

(Sings.)
Here I comes
With me bucket of bums
Isn't it a lovely day?

I live in the slums
With a posh set of drums
That I never have time to play.

I've got double-jointed thumbs
And receding gums
But otherwise I'm OK.

And when I meet my chums

Walking out with their mums
This is what I always say —

Here I comes
With me bucket of bums
Isn't it a lovely day?

Cheerio. Keep smiling.

(Waves to SOLDIER and exits.)

MISS ROVER: There's the London Demolition Company. They're doing very well.

CONDUCTRESS (to SOLDIER): Money, please.

SOLDIER: Shaftesbury Theatre?

CONDUCTRESS: That's the next stop.

SOLDIER: Going to see that show *Hair.* I've never seen a live nude before.

CONDUCTRESS: Too late, love. Show's over.

SOLDIER: What happened?

CONDUCTRESS: Roof fell in.

SOLDIER: Just my bloody luck. Have to go and see one of them religious shows. Jesus and the Technicolor Beanstalk. Hey, you give any reduction for randy soldiers?

CONDUCTRESS: Randy soldiers are free. But we charge double for guns.

SOLDIER: But I'm going overseas.

(Bus stops.)

CONDUCTRESS: Can't you find anyone to shoot in England?

SOLDIER (paying, getting off bus): Look, I wanted to be a farmer. Useless. Couldn't even afford a window box. Land costs three hundred quid an acre. Buy me a farm, and I'll go back, love. You think I like this bloody gun?

CONDUCTRESS (ringing bell twice): Nothing personal, son. Mind your head.

MISS ROVER: Bloomsbury. James Smith and Sons. Swordsticks. Riding crops and whips. Dagger Canes and Life Preservers.

(DRIVER gets out, runs back, beckons to CONDUCTRESS. She gets out impatiently. A relaxed FREAK appears beside them and listens. In this Act FREAK is pleasant and natural.)

DRIVER: Mother, I've got to tell you something. Urgent.

CONDUCTRESS: What's the trouble?

DRIVER: I can't look at you.

CONDUCTRESS: I'm not that grotesque.

DRIVER: No, I mean I can look at you. But when I do, I don't see you. There's something in the way. And when I try to speak to you, my tongue won't move. I can't tell you the truth, there's iron railings between us. Iron railings. Spikes along the top, can't climb over. Iron railings. So close together I can't see between them. I'm sorry. I'll shut up.

(FREAK emerges from BAND with guitar.)

FREAK: If you can use it, I've got a spell to make a bad time pass.

CONDUCTRESS: If you're our fairy godfather, let's see you turn this bugger

(Indicating bus.)

into a pumpkin.

DRIVER: Magic!

(To audience.)

Clap hands if you believe in Uri Geller. How about Tommy Cooper then?

FREAK: You don't have to call it a spell. It's just an exercise.

CONDUCTRESS: That's different.

DRIVER: Exercise is different.

FREAK: OK, sit down.

(They sit.)

To make a bad time pass, this is what you do.

(DRIVER and CONDUCTRESS follow his instructions.)

FREAK (sings):
> Unfold your hand
>
> Put all the bad times
> In the palm of your hand
>
> Slowly close your fingers
> To make a gentle fist
>
> Slowly turn your fist around
> Let your eyes move slowly
> Over the surface of your fist
>
> Slowly turn your fist around
> Let your lips pass slowly
> Over the surface of your fist
>
> Slowly
> Tighten your fingers
> Slowly
> Tighten your fist
>
> Your fist is clenched
> All the bad times are inside it
> Your fist is clenched

All the bad times are vanishing

Slowly, slowly
Unfold the fingers of your hand

The palm of your hand is empty

Look into the palm of your hand
Look deep into your hand

Your hand is full
Your hand is full
Your hand is full of life.

CONDUCTRESS: That's a pretty one.

DRIVER: I feel a bit better. Hasn't changed the world though, has it?

FREAK (rejoining BAND): No, that takes real work.

(DRIVER, back in cab, starts bus again.)

MISS ROVER: Angus Steak House. Greater London Parks Department. Patriotism is not enough. I must have no hatred or bitterness towards anyone. There's Nelson. I'm sure he wouldn't approve of those demonstrators. Nelson was small, but he was a great hero. I am Sexy and Erotic Blue. Whitehall. British Union for the Abolition of Vivisection. Loretta's Soft Ice Cream. The Glorious Dead.

(HORACE HAMPTON, an impresario, unrolls a zebra crossing in front of the bus, then drives MAHALIA SMITH on to it with a stick. MAHALIA is totally encased in a sacklike costume except for one eye and her mouth. Bus screeches to a halt.)

DRIVER (to HORACE): What in the name of crimson creation do you think you're doing?

HORACE: Just a little technique I've devised in order to bring buses to heel.

DRIVER: A bus is not a poodle. Out of my way.

HORACE: Say please.

DRIVER: Please, bloody please.

(HORACE and MAHALIA move off crossing and on to lower deck.)

HORACE (to MAHALIA): Failure! Failure! All you do is fail! A star is supposed to shine. Shine! Right. Do I get you auditions? I get you auditions. And do you shine? Do you? No, you just sit on the stage like a hump of sulk.

(DRIVER starts up. Then stops as BISCUITS BEIDERBECKE, a cheerful old man in oil skins and sou'wester, crosses crossing and up to upper deck. DRIVER starts again, has to stop as JELLY-ROLL HOLIDAY, prostitute, crosses and up the stairs. DRIVER starts. INSPECTOR appears on crossing. DRIVER stops, starts, stops again.)

DRIVER: I can't do it. Not on a zebra crossing. Not right by the Cenotaph.

The Glorious Dead.

CONDUCTRESS: Fares please.

HORACE: One bloodytory impresario and one disabled star to Victoria Street.

CONDUCTRESS: One twenty p and one for free.

(DRIVER gets out of cab and up to INSPECTOR.)

DRIVER: You come most carefully upon your hour.

INSPECTOR: Mussolini made the trains run on time. I do the same for the buses.

(Mounts bus.)

DRIVER (tucking crossing under his arm and mounting cab): This'll look nice on the bathroom floor. When I get a bathroom.

INSPECTOR (to HORACE): Let's see 'em.

(HORACE proffers tickets. INSPECTOR looks at them.)

HORACE: It's a strange thing, but you remind me of someone, name's on the tip of my tongue, don't tell me.

INSPECTOR: Oh yes, I'm always being mistaken for him –

(Sings like Satchmo.)
     I see buses of red
     Under skies of blue
     Trafalgar's square
     And so are you
     And I think to myself
     What a wonderful world . . .

Oh yes, we're related on my father's side.

HORACE: Fascinating – I'm in show business myself. Let me tell you . . .

(HORACE and INSPECTOR enter into silent friendly conversation. Upstairs for fares.)

MISS ROVER: There's Big Ben. It's always right. And a big yellow bull-dozer in the MP's car park. Surely they're not going to knock down the Houses of Parliament to build a motorway? I'm the Red Rover.

CONDUCTRESS: What's yours?

JELLYROLL: The usual, dear.

CONDUCTRESS (giving ticket): One all-day Gooser Special.

JELLYROLL: Ta.

MISS ROVER: Martini Rossi. Wealthy people with private seaplanes drink it. Perhaps I would be less nervous of people if I drank Martini Rossi.

BISCUITS: Could you oblige me by telling me the serial number of the next ticket?

JELLYROLL (looking at ticket): 234.

BISCUITS (quick calculation): Marvellous, marvellous. I'll take 144 5p tickets please.

(Produces note. CONDUCTRESS begins to zip off 144 tickets, which roll down the stairs in a stream.)

BISCUITS: 144 will take me to number 378. A particularly lucky number for me.

JELLYROLL: You're fond of bus tickets?

BISCUITS: Hardly. But I'm Professor of Omnibusology at the University of Lundy Island.

JELLYROLL: I didn't know there was a university on Lundy.

BISCUITS: Well, university is a slight exaggeration. Actually there's only me. And a few puffins.

JELLYROLL: Puffins are pretty.

BISCUITS: But not very practical. Anyway, I run a correspondence school for potential busmen. And my pupils send me bus tickets with rare or curious numbers.

JELLYROLL: If the numbers on a chap's ticket add up to 21 he puts it down the back of a girl's neck if he fancies her. Down the front if he wants to marry her.

BISCUITS: What if she doesn't like him?

JELLYROLL: She sticks it up his arse. Do they do that on Lundy buses?

BISCUITS: Actually there aren't any buses on Lundy. In fact this is my very first journey on a bus, but buses are basic to my philosophic thesis. Life, I always say, is like a double-decker bus.

CONDUCTRESS: You always say that?

BISCUITS: Almost continuously. We are born, that is we get on the bus. We travel a little way, we pay our fare, and then we are set down in death.

CONDUCTRESS: But we don't choose where we get on, do we?

BISCUITS: But we do. On the route of Destiny, birth and death are request stops. When you were a little sperm in your father's scrotum, you woke one day with a sudden urge to fertilise. Today's the day, you said to yourself. Today I'm going to enter the big race. I'll sprint up the vagina, take the inside track round the fallopian tubes and beat all the others to the egg. And by George, you did. You won!

JELLYROLL: What a nice old man you are. Now I understand it all. Life is a bus. But who is the driver?

CONDUCTRESS (giving BISCUITS his tickets): My son Owen.

(She goes downstairs.)

BISCUITS: I'm a very excited old man today.

JELLYROLL: Well it's a bumpy surface down Victoria Street.

BISCUITS: No — my very first bus ride. But tell me, if that was the conductress, who are you? And why did you sell me this scarlet ticket?

JELLYROLL: That entitled you to what we call a bus job.

BISCUITS: But I'm self-employed.

JELLYROLL: You've paid your fare. Read your ticket.

(JELLYROLL kneels in front of him, unzips his flies and lowers her face into his lap under his oilskin.)

BISCUITS: The whore of the upper deck invites you to lean back and relax. Not Transferable.

MISS ROVER: Neathouse Place. I could do with a Brunchburger.

BISCUITS: D'you mind if I sing?

(JELLYROLL shakes her head.)

Outside the cottage where I was raised on Lundy, there was a big green waterbutt with a brass tap. I spent so many happy hours playing with that tub when I was a boy —

(Sings emotionally — Jolson style:)

Oh that tub!
That grand old wooden tub!
I want to see that grand old tub again!
Oh that tub!
Underneath the rainpipe
Filling up, on rainy days, with rain!

No, I'll never forget!
Yes, I'll always remember!
Whether it's rain or shine —
The feeling I get,
May or December,
Dreaming of that grand old tub of mine!

What's that you say?
You saw my tub?
Tell me where and I'll go there
Though it were upon the furthest star!
What's that you say?
The city dump?
Broken up? No, I'm not sad —
Must've been the smoke from your cigar . . .

Oh my tub!
My grand old wooden tub!
I'll make up for all they've done to you.
Just you wait,
I won't be late —

I'm going to fix you up like new!
'Cause I've got paint and I've got glue!

Oh that tub!
You grand old wooden tub!
I'm coming back! We'll always be together!
Oh you tub!
Tub! Tub! Tub! Tuuuuuuuuuuuuuuuuuuub!

Thank you. That's the nicest thing anyone's ever done for me.

JELLYROLL: Meals on wheels, that's what it is. I'm a kind of freelance social worker.

DRIVER (over loudspeaker): Come down here and do some work on a problem area.

JELLYROLL: Sorry love, I can't seem to fancy it.

DRIVER: Why not?

JELLYROLL: The uniform plays some part in it, I think.

DRIVER: I'm beginning to think that the *News of the World* is over-imaginative.

MISS ROVER: Belgrave Road — Luna House Hotel, Simone House Hotel, Corona Hotel. Beverly Towers, that sounds smart. I wonder if any of them have swimming pools. I would like to sit beside a hotel swimming pool. Lunches served to non-residents. What a good idea.

(Getting up and leaving bus.)

I'll spoil myself with a non-resident lunch. Wonder if they let you keep the menu. These stairs are very steep. I expect old people have to go down backwards. After lunch I shall catch another bus. My Red Rover will still be valid.

CONDUCTRESS: Why is it you read out the street names and the writing on buildings? Is it because you're lonely?

MISS ROVER: Why don't you shut up?

(Exit MISS ROVER.)

INSPECTOR: May I see your tickets? One bloody tory impresario, right. And one disabled star? What's the disablement?

HORACE: Actually, Inspector, she's the ugliest girl in the world. Really horrific. That's why she has to be covered up like this.

INSPECTOR: I shall consult my book of rules. There are many rules.

HORACE: Don't be hard on her, officer. We've had a bad day. She just failed an audition at the Talk of the Town.

CONDUCTRESS: What's her act?

INSPECTOR: Yes, does she strip off that sack to show how disgustingly ugly she is?

HORACE: Couldn't do that, out of the question. Clear the theatre in two minutes flat. Clear it for good. No, she just sits there and answers questions from Michael Aspel about how does it feel to be the Ugliest Girl in the world.

INSPECTOR (leafing through rule book): That does not count as a disability. Extreme ugliness does not count.

HORACE: You've caught me red-handed, squire. Look, I told you a white lie. For the girl's own protection. Don't tell the others, but she's the most Beautiful Girl in the world. That's her disablement. She's such an impossibly stimulating vision of pulchritude that last time I let her out in a trouser suit, the Oxford Street area was converted into two square miles of writhing and groping naked citizens.

INSPECTOR: Allow me to confirm your story.

CONDUCTRESS: Claud! Not on the morning after our wedding night.

INSPECTOR: Just one official glance, Myfanwy.

(DRIVER stops bus. Gets out, round to lower saloon.)

DRIVER: My sixth sense tells me that the most Beautiful Girl in the world is on this bus.

HORACE: And here she is son. A sight to make a eunuch slobber.

DRIVER (calls upstairs): Hey, we've got the most beautiful girl in the world on board. Come and see.

(JELLYROLL and BISCUITS come downstairs to see.)

INSPECTOR: I am afraid that this passenger is in breach of the regulations, sir. No disguise allowed on buses. Otherwise we'd be getting bank robbers, spies and fugitive Nazi leaders swarming all over our number 24s. Remove that bizarre garb at once.

HORACE: If you insist, sir. It'll cost you a fiver.

(INSPECTOR tears open the top of the sack, looks in. The others look in. They close the top of the sack. MAHALIA comes forward.)

MAHALIA:
The outside of my body was half-eaten
by the fire which clings as tight as skin.
The fire has turned some of my skin
into black scab bits of roughness
and some pale bits, smooth as plastic,
which no one dares touch
except me and the doctor.

Everyone who looks at me is scared.
That's not because I want to hurt people
but because so much of me
looks like the meat of a monster.

I was walking to the Market.
Then I was screaming.
They found me screaming.
They put out the flames on my skin.
They laid me on a stretcher and I cried:
Not on my back!
So they turned me over and I cried:
Not on my front!

A doctor put a needle in my arm
and my mind melted
and I fell into a furnace of dreams of furnaces.

When I woke up I was in a white hospital.
Everything I wanted to say scared me
and I did not want to scare the others
in that white hospital
so I said nothing, cried as quietly as I could.

Months passed over my head
and bombers passed over my head
and people came and said they were my parents
and they found out the places on my face
where I could bear to be kissed.

And I pretended I could see them
but I couldn't really look out of my eyes
but only inwards, into my head
where the flames still clung and hurt, and talked.

And the flames said:
You are meat.
You are ugly meat.
Your body cannot heal to loveliness.
Nobody could love such ugly meat.
Only ugly meat could love such ugly meat.
Better be stewed for soup and eaten.

And months passed over my head
and bombers passed over my head
and the voices of the flames began to flicker
and I began to believe
the people who said they were my parents
were my parents.

And one day I threw myself forward
so that I sat up in bed, for the first time,
and hurled my arms around my mother,
and however the skin of my chest howled out its pain
I held her, I held her, I held her
and knew she was my mother.
And I forgot that I was monster meat

And knew she did not know that I was monster meat.

I held her, I held her.

And, sweet sun which blesses all the world —
all the flames faded.
The flames of my skin
and the flames inside my head —
all the flames faded
and I was flooded
with love for my mother
who did not know
that I was monster meat.

And so, in the love-flood, I let go of my mother
and fell back on my pillow
and I rolled my head to the left side
and saw a child, or it might have been an old man,
eating his rice with his only arm
and I rolled my head to the right side
and saw another child, or she might have been an old woman
being fed through the arm from a tube from a red bottle —
and I loved them, and, flooded with love
I started to sing
the song of the game I used to play with my friends
in the long-ago days before the flames came:

(Sings.)

One, one, bounce the ball.
Once for the sandal-maker.
Two, two, bounce the ball.
Twice for the fisherman on the river.
Three, three, bounce the ball.
Three times for your golden lover.

(Speaks.)

And had to stop singing.
Throat choked with vomit.
And then the flames exploded again all over my skin
and then the flames exploded again inside my head
and I burned, sweet sun, sweet mother, I burned.

(MAHALIA turns her back. CONDUCTRESS and JELLYROLL go to her.)

CONDUCTRESS: Hospital, love. We'll get you back to hospital.

INSPECTOR: Not nice. Not nice on a bus.

JELLYROLL: Rotten pimp, trying to turn you into a freak show.

CONDUCTRESS: Hospital, love.

(CONDUCTRESS and JELLYROLL take her out, followed by BISCUITS.)

INSPECTOR (to HORACE): I'm afraid you'll have to accompany me to the depot sir. That was an illegal immigrant if ever I saw one.

HORACE: But she's my bread and butter.

INSPECTOR (leading HORACE out): This way, sir.

> (DRIVER is left alone.)

DRIVER: I suppose we love each other. We're stupid if we don't. A weird species, we are. Some of us choking to death on our own vomit. Some of us more like the sweet sun, which blesses all the world.

> (Sings.)
> I was looking through a book of photos
> Called something like the face of mankind
> And as I turned the pages of faces
> Their pictures got printed on my mind
>
> Because there were no ordinary people
> They all looked different to me.
> Well there are no ordinary people
> Every human being is extraordinary.
>
> And there's no other pebble like you
> Among the millions on the beach
> So there's no single message for everyone
> We need a thousand messages each.
>
> Some of the messages are comic
> Some of the messages are sad
> Some of the messages are pretty little daisies
> And some are monstrous and mad.

> (Speaks.)

> And one of the messages is this:

> (Sings.)
> The worst thing in the world
> The worst thing in the world
> The worst thing in the world
> Is what some people
> Do to other people
>
> Yes I know
> The best thing in the world
> The best thing in the world
> The best thing in the world
> Is what some people
> Do for other people
>
> But
> The worst thing in the world
> The worst thing in the world
> The worst thing in the world
> Is what some people
> Do to other people.

> (DRIVER exits.)

# ACT TWO

The VIKING has been guarding the bus during the interval, reading a slim volume to pass the time. As houselights dim, he comes forward. The roller on the front of the bus now reads:

24  VICTORIA
WHITEHALL
CHARING CROSS ROAD
HAMPSTEAD ROAD
CAMDEN TOWN
HAMPSTEAD HEATH

VIKING: I have been enjoying your English interval with this book – *Best Viking Buzz Yokes*. You would care for a Viking Buzz Yoke? At your service.

(He reads, with difficulty in concealing his mirth, *one* of the following:)

1.  A Viking buzzman was delivering a veteran buzz to a scrapyard beside a remote fijord when his vehicle broke down outside a farmhouse. The farmer invited the buzzman to eat, and a meal was brought by the farmer's buxom wife and his beautiful daughter. After dinner the buzzman asked: 'Do you think you could let me sleep here tonight?' 'I'm afraid not,' said the farmer, 'we don't have a spare room. But there is a perfectly good boarding-house down the road and I'm sure they can put you up!'

2.  An American buzzman, a Russian buzzman, a Jewish buzzman, an English buzzman and a Viking buzzman were driving to Tromso when their buzz broke down. The American changed the water, the Russian checked the oil, the Jew changed one of the wheels, the Englishman tested the engine and the Viking phoned to report the incident to the depot at Tromso!

3.  This is a riddle from the back of one of our Viking matchboxes.
    Question:   What is the difference between a herringboat and a buzz
                conductress on the West Coast of Norway?
    Answer:     A herringboat is a fishing vessel and a buzz conductress on
                the West Coast of Norway is a Bergen clippie!

4.  When a buzzdriver and his bride arrived at their honeymoon hotel in Narvik, the pretty blonde receptionist asked them to sign the Visitors' Book. 'I'm sorry,' said the groom, 'but I seem to have mislaid my pen!' 'Here you are sir, you can borrow this one!' was the receptionist's pert response.

5.  Two buzzmen from Trondheim and Oslo were boasting about their responsibilities. 'Last year my buzz carried 12,464 passengers,' claimed the Trondheim driver. 'That's nothing,' retorted his companion, 'mine

carried 14,922!'

6. A conductor on the route between Andalsnes and Hamar was surprised when a red-haired man offered to pay his fare in oat-cakes rather than coins. The conductor refused. Next day a black-haired man got on the bus and proffered two home-made candles in exchange for his ticket. Again the bemused conductor refused. The day after that a white-haired man boarded the buzz with his wife and two sons and paid their exact fares in cash!

7. A buzz inspector from Lillehammer boarded a buzz at Grimstad, bent down, picked something off the platform, stared at it, then threw it off the buzz. 'What was that?' inquired the conductress. 'I don't know, said the inspector. 'Then why did you throw it off the buzz?' she queried. The inspector sighed before making this devastating rejoinder: 'I threw it off the buzz because I didn't know what it was!'

(*NOTE:* The VIKING is invited to make up some Viking Buzz Yokes of his own for use on different evenings. *Rules:* 1. A Viking Buzz Yoke always sounds like a joke, but has no pay-off. 2. It always concerns buses or busmen in some way. 3. It is always set in Norway. Useful Norwegian placenames – Alesund, Drammen, Sor Trondelag, Trollheimen, Stavanger, Telemark, Kroken and Fokstad.)

You will observe that the Viking Buzz Yoke differs from the English Buzz Yoke in one respect. The English buzz yoke is an anecdote ending in a pay-off line, which is known as – the point of the yoke. The Viking Buzz Yoke is an anecdote ending in a full stop. Another specimen.

(Reads another joke.)

These yokes are part of the Viking heritage. But let's get on with the story. It is now the evening of the same day. The bus is about to perform its return journey from Pimlico to Hampstead. Most people are returning from work, but not the band, who are on their way to another jig –

MUSICIANS: Gig!

VIKING: Another engagement in Hampstead.

(Enter DRIVER.)

Had a rewarding day, Owen? How's it been?

DRIVER: Well it started out when I got a new bus, this bent one with a band on board. And my mother told me she's married my uncle. Oh yes, and I met my father's ghost and he made me swear to kill my uncle. But I'm not sure that my uncle really is my uncle. I'd say it's been a pretty average day, so far.

VIKING: Nothing unusual to report?

DRIVER: Let's see. Yes. Almost everybody I met today – they've been telling the truth about themselves, telling the truth. Except Claud. And me.

VIKING (excited): Well, munuc hatte abbo, Owen.

DRIVER: Mind your helmet.

> (Enter CONDUCTRESS, who gives DRIVER a kiss as she passes.)

> Hey, what was that for Mum?

CONDUCTRESS: 'Cos I love you.

> (Gets on bus, humming to herself.)

DRIVER: She's on Bacardi tonight. I don't know that she ought to say that she loves me, me being her son. I don't know . . .

> (Enter SCHOOLGIRL — bright red uniform beret, red blazer, red shoes. She gropes DRIVER as she passes.)

DRIVER: Excuse me, miss, but you wouldn't be the Netherley Nymph would you?

SCHOOLGIRL: Listen, wage-slave, I'm going to tell you exactly who I am.

> (Takes up aggressive stance with MUSICIANS. Sings, dances, aggressive Jagger style.)

> I'm the little red schoolgirl, I've got a head that's all my own.
> I'm the little red schoolgirl, I've got a head that's all my own.
> If you want to reach retirement, better leave my little red mind alone.

> You taught me 'bout equations and what the Romans used to do,
> Embroidery and cookery — bloody netball too.
> If you started teaching freedom, I might begin to listen to you.

> 'Cos I'm the little red schoolgirl, I wasn't born to be no bride.
> I'm the little red schoolgirl, on that helter-skelter slide.
> Hey little grey headmaster, you'd better step quickly aside.

> Had a dream that I saw freedom, gonna grab just as much as I can
> Got my hands full of freedom, freedom is my loving man.

> 'Cos I'm the little red schoolgirl, no teacher can turn me round.
> Yes I'm the little red schoolgirl, parents can't turn me round.
> Now I'm making out with freedom, and the schools come tumbling down.
> Now I'm making out with freedom, and the schools come tumbling down.

> (Enter BUMBO GILLESPIE, a smooth TV compère. He takes her microphone.)

BUMBO: What a lovely little girl! That's certainly one for the Eurovision Song Contest.

SCHOOLGIRL: Who the hell are you?

BUMBO: A television personality.

SCHOOLGIRL: Then I'm riding on a different bus.

> (Exit.)

BUMBO: Good evening, ladies and gentlemen, this is your happy host, Bumbo Gillespie, introducing another session of your favourite public transport quiz — That's The Ticket!

(MUSICIANS do big chord.)

And tonight's transport of delight comes from a bus on the number 24 route at Lupus Street, Pimlico, LONDON. Let's hear it for the Number 24 route. And now I'd like to introduce the two learned teams.

(Enter CONDON MELLY, very drunk man, and MAN KENTON, wearing scuba suit carrying flippers. They both go to top deck and sit facing audience. Also HOLLY TEAGARDEN, low-cut, grinning housewife in her best clothes, who sits on the lower deck, below KENTON. CONDUC-TRESS is sitting, by chance, below MELLY.)

Now the first of our contestants is —

CONDON (nudged by MAN): Feeling a bit.

BUMBO: Your name sir?

CONDON: Condo — Condon Melly.

BUMBO: And your occupation?

CONDON: Drunkest man in the world.

BUMBO: How about that folks? And his team-mate is —

MAN (ingratiatingly): Man Kenton's the name. I sell self-insurance.

BUMBO: Self-insurance. Sounds good, but how does it work?

MAN: Depends on your policy. I can insure you against anything you do to yourself. Self-mutilation, self-immolation, self-abuse. But naturally the biggest market is for insurance against suicide.

BUMBO: Great. Great. Let's hear it for the self! Mr Kenton may I ask why are you wearing a scuba suit?

MAN: As you know, the insurance business thrives on fear. I wear this cumbersome costume in order to prod your subconscious fear of water to a point where you will buy insurance against drowning.

BUMBO: Thank you very much. Excuse me.

(BUMBO dashes off-stage.)

HOLLY: Well, my name's Holly Teagarden and I'm a contented housewife. My hobby is housework and I'm so contented that I often think I've died and gone to heaven.

(BUMBO returns.)

BUMBO (to CONDUCTRESS): Your name Madam?

CONDUCTRESS: Myfanwy Stubber — oh no!

BUMBO: Oh yes. Myfanwy! You are the surprise expert on this week's That's The Ticket —

CONDUCTRESS: Got no time for quizzes.

BUMBO: And little Myfanwy is an actual bus conductress!

CONDUCTRESS: Only contest I do is Spot the Ball.

BUMBO: What a delicious sense of humour!

HOLLY: My husband has a delicious sense of humour. Every Saturday night he slips a pound note under my pillow.

BUMBO: Right, now, let's get on with the quiz.

(FOUR CONTESTANTS sit up and finger buzzers.)

BUMBO: Now here's your starter for ten. How would you distinguish between an RT bus and an RTL? Yes, Mr Kenton?

MAN: Partly by the design of the radiator and also by the harsher note of the RTL's engine and its vigorous throb when idling.

BUMBO: That's exactly what I've got written down here.

(Bell.)

Next question. What unusual incident occurred on route 78 in the post war years? Yes, Mrs Holly Teagarden.

HOLLY: It was on, um, December 13th, 1952. The bus was RT 793 operating from Dalston Garage. Evening trip going south over Tower Bridge. But half-way across the bridge, the section the bus was on started to rise. Making a split-second decision, the driver elected to jump the widening gap onto the other bascule, which remained in the horizontal position. It landed on the stationary bascule after a drop of about three feet. The crew and twelve of the twenty passengers were slightly injured.

(Bell.)

BUMBO: Well that was quite an easy one. Now we'll – excuse me a minute.

(BUMBO off. All freeze in acute embarrassment.)

DRIVER (to CONDUCTRESS): Why's he keep nipping off like that?

(BUMBO returns.)

BUMBO: Now let's have a few quickies. What were the average fuel returns on the RT bus in 1956?

MAN: 9.5 miles per gallon in Central London, 10.5 in the Country areas.

(Bell.)

Each vehicle, incidentally was equipped with a 35 gallon fuel tank.

BUMBO: Just answer the question. Of all the RTW buses, the eight-foot-wide buses authorized for general use in June 1946, one was the odd man out.

CONDON (turgidly through drunken haze): Yeah, that'd be RTW 375. Instead of having the conventional fluid flywheel and preselective gearbox, it received pneumocyclic semi-automatic transmission, necessitating the use of only two pedals.

(Bell.)

BUMBO: That's the ticket!

(Chord from MUSICIANS.)

Who or what is BESI?

CONDUCTRESS: Bessie Smith — greatest blues singer in the world.

BUMBO: No.

(Raucous horn noise.)

CONDUCTRESS: She bloody is.

(Sulks.)

BUMBO: B.E.S.I. is —

ALL: Bus Electronic Scanning Indicator.

(Bell.)

BUMBO: Right. Name a bus which starred in a film.

HOLLY: RT 2305, 2366 and 4326 all appeared in the Cliff Richard film *Summer Holiday.*

(Bell.)

BUMBO: Correct. Name thirteen bus companies which started in London during the 1920s.

MAN: Triumph, Matchless, Criterion, Eclipse, Empire's Best, Pioneer, New Era, Renown, Supreme, Uneedus, Nil Desperandum, Pro Bono Publico and Pickup.

(Bell.)

BUMBO: Yes, pardon me.

(BUMBO exits.)

HOLLY: I don't see why we should sit here pardoning him.

CONDON: Pardon?

MAN: Let's confront him when he comes back.

(BUMBO returns.)

You confront him.

CONDON: Where you going all the time? One moment you're here then you piss off then you piss back then you piss off again.

BUMBO: Well, that's it. That's why I lost my late-night chat show and got reduced to bus quizzes. Weak bladder. I'd sit down with distinguished guests like Norman Mailer and President Nixon and Jilly Cooper, and then wham, I'd have to zip out for a piddle. In fact I had to go out so often that the public had no opportunity to become familiar with my face and that's no way to establish yourself as a TV personality. Well, that's my problem. Now it's — Question Time!

(GLUEPOT OLIVER rises from the audience.)

GLUEPOT: I would like to bring up —

BUMBO: Speak up. Name please?

GLUEPOT: Gluepot Oliver. My organization is concerned about the labelling of buses.

BUMBO: What organization is that?

GLUEPOT: NOESP.

(Spits the P.)

NOESP.

BUMBO: Come?

GLUEPOT: The National Organization of Extremely Stupid People. I am an extremely stupid person and I think I speak for all extremely stupid people when I say that all buses should bear an explanatory label.

BUMBO: And what should be written on the label?

GLUEPOT: Well extremely stupid people have difficulty in recognizing buses. Only last week I myself climbed on an oak tree thinking that it was a number nine bus —

BUMBO: So what would you like written on the side of buses?

GLUEPOT: Simply the word bus. Just B — U — G. So everyone knows it's a bus.

CONDUCTRESS: I don't see any need for a bus to say it's a bus.

GLUEPOT: I see, you're ashamed of your bus. You're afraid of calling a bus a bus.

DRIVER: Look you don't have people walking around with labels on them saying Man or Woman do you?

GLUEPOT: That's the first constructive suggestion I've heard tonight. I'll buy a label for myself tomorrow saying MAN OR WOMAN.

CONDUCTRESS: You're extremely stupid.

GLUEPOT: And proud of it. Just a minute. I'll think of a witty comeback to that. I know. You — have got a face — like the back — of a bus.

DRIVER: Right, that does it.

(DRIVER thumps GLUEPOT.)

BUMBO (to Viewers): The driver is now thumping the extremely stupid person who has just insulted his mother.

DRIVER: Mother be punctured. He sneered at my bus.

BUMBO: Break. Break!

(DRIVER chases GLUEPOT out.)

Terribly sorry about that. Teething troubles with access to the medium. But now back to the show. I'd like to introduce our guest artiste — the latest rock sensation — The Stone Ground Freak!

(FREAK enters. Since Act One he has become super-trendy.)

FREAK: Hi! Hi! And the higher the finer. Cats and kitties, prepare to worship, because I'm going to blow your minds like bubble-gum bubbles —

CONDUCTRESS: Hey, aren't you the nice young man who was telling us how to get rid of bad times this morning?

FREAK: This morning was years ago, babydoll. I was discovered at lunchtime. By cocktail time I was a superstar.

CONDUCTRESS: Will we be seeing you again?

FREAK: On all three channels.

BUMBO: The viewers, the viewers are waiting Stone Ground.

(DRIVER returns.)

FREAK: Beautiful, that is beautiful.

(Sings the following cut-up headlines from *Oz Magazine* with intense showmanship.)
>Smile if you had sex last night.
>Hey, you know any place I can crash?
>Would-be leaders shoot on sight
>But first I've got to get my stash.
>
>We'll turn the lower east side
>Into a woodland glade.
>You know a man must make his move
>Before his move is made
>And every home should have one
>Every home should have one.
>
>Jessie was a Trotskyite —
>Well, you are what you eat.
>But summer's here and the time is right
>For dancing in the street.
>
>Do it again like a nation on heat.
>Keef is the working man's drummer.
>Jelly roll gum drops are good to eat.
>The missionary position is a bummer
>But every home should have one
>Every home should have one.
>
>Who did Jagger ever kill?
>Dear Doctor Hippocrates,
>I need five dozen ampules
>Of amyl nitrate please.
>
>There's a shmuck in the tall dark hallway
>Blinded by tear gas and mace,

But whoring along the Hudson
We'll win the human race
And every home should have one
Every home should have one.

We were dragged to the place of sacrifice
By Honeybunch Kamensky.
I have seen the bird of paradise,
She has spread her wings before me.

I yelled: I agree with your tactics,
But I don't know about your goal.
But she called the Church of Anthrax
And the merciless mayhem patrol.
Every home should have one
Every home should have one.

When the mode of the music changes
The walls of the city shake.
Fortify the over forties —
They've arrested a birthday cake.

Mr Freedom has the big one
Down on the sewage farm.
Put a real queen in the palace,
The Madonna of Napalm.
Every home should have one,
Every home should have one.

Search for your brothers and sisters.
Mind your head, mind your head.
If they offer you insurance —
Strike them dead.

If you make a revolution
Make it for fun.
You're part of the problem or part of the solution —
Men, it can be done!
And every home should have one,
Every home should have one
Every home should have one.

(DRIVER jumps out of his cab, runs to CONDUCTRESS.)

DRIVER: Get those lights out of here, they're melting the Red Revenger.

BUMBO: Break. Break.

DRIVER: My heart is in the clutches of a clandestine passion, and you
allow this acid-dropping parody of the great Bob Dylan to commandeer
my bus. Hey, and that song of yours — it's nothing but a lot of headlines
chopped out of *Oz Magazine* and stuck together with fish-glue.

FREAK: You are correct. You must have quadrophonic ears. How'd you like to write some really laid-back sleeve notes for my new album?

DRIVER: I'll lay the lot of you back if you don't exit sharpish.

BUMBO: Show must go on.

DRIVER: London Transport must go on.

BUMBO: OK. Everyone take five. Take five hundred and five.

(TV people exit. Enter INSPECTOR.)

INSPECTOR: Hold your horse-power. Aren't you forgetting what day it is today?

DRIVER: Friday? Monday? Wednesday? All days look alike to me until I enjoy my great Revenge.

INSPECTOR: Take a shufti in the Busman's Diary.

(CONDUCTRESS produces big red diary in the shape of a bus, takes it to DRIVER. They study it.)

It is an invaluable almanac of anniversaries and public events. Quite apart from its intriguing statistics about Argentinian bus routes and pen-portraits of leading Viennese trolley-drivers.

CONDUCTRESS: Tercentenary of the Sedan Chair?

DRIVER: No, here it is. On this date the number 24 at Lupus Street, Pimlico, will be honoured by a — Royal Visit.

INSPECTOR: Right.

(Shouts.)

Attention. Royal Visit. Everybody off!

(ALL PASSENGERS begin to leave, DRIVER, INSPECTOR and CONDUCTRESS spring into action. CONDUCTRESS sweeps. DRIVER polishes, INSPECTOR inspects. They don gold jackets with medals. INSPECTOR has Iron Cross — and golden ticket machine for CONDUCTRESS. INSPECTOR lines up DRIVER and CONDUCTRESS and inspects them. Roller changes to Union Jack and God Save the Queen upside down. Enter QUEEN ELIZABETH II on REGAL PANTOMIME HORSE, dragging stuffed corgis on wheels.)

QUEEN: This visit to a lowly omnibus will further cement our ties with the so-called working classes. Therefore, we would alight.

INSPECTOR: Allow me mighty Monarchess.

(QUEEN alights.)

QUEEN: Tell me Inspector, am I beloved by the masses on the buses?

INSPECTOR: Love is too bold a word, Majesty, to compass it.
Do sheep presume to love their shepherd? Or do pigs
Presume a passion for their swineherd?

Rather say — that in a stupor of devoted bliss
The workers are as lugworms to your radiance.

QUEEN (aside): Methinks that's worth an MBE at least.

INSPECTOR (rising): Your Majesty — observe a pageant of great London's transport.

(A pageant of buses, trolleys etc. passes to music.)

And now your Majesty, here is a brave Conductress.

QUEEN: I envy thee thy lot.

CONDUCTRESS: Well you can have it.

QUEEN (to DRIVER): The driver of the bus?

INSPECTOR: He is, your Majesty.

QUEEN (to DRIVER): Tell me young man, what passes through your mind as you convey our subjects here and there?

DRIVER (passionately): I think about my mother —

QUEEN: How nice —

DRIVER: And contemplate my great Revenge.

INSPECTOR (producing champagne bottle): Your Majesty, 'tis time to launch the bus.

QUEEN (nods and produces script; sotto voce): Wonder what they've given me this time.

(From script.)

In this age of the exploration of space, the discovery of the double helix, the tapping of the oil resources of the North Atlantic Ocean and the growth of the Ecumenical Movement in our Churches, I wonder how many of us ever stop and think and ask ourselves this question: how often do I violate the environment by thoughtlessly disposing of my bus ticket? Every bus, after all, is provided with a bin for used tickets.

(A VULGAR PANTO STALLION enters, spots REGAL PANTO HORSE, sidles round it amorously and begins to copulate with it.)

Now one little bus ticket may seem to us a petty object when we compare it with the exploration of space, the discovery of the double Helix, the tapping of the oil resources of the North Atlantic Ocean and the growth of the Ecumenical Movement in our Churches. But I wonder how many of us ever stop and think and say to ourselves: a rutting stallion appears to have penetrated my mount!

(Exit QUEEN and HORSES. Roller back to normal.)

INSPECTOR: Your Majesty, the launching! You haven't blessed the bus.

(Exit INSPECTOR.)

CONDUCTRESS (opening champagne bottle and swigging): Getting married makes you sleepy.

DRIVER: My fingers are trembling and the veins on the back of my hands are all blue and bulging. That usually means I've fallen in love. I can't remember doing that today. But only love turns me so nervy. It always has done. When I was thirteen, if a girl had touched me with love, I'd have jumped six feet into the air. Yes, and I'd have achieved an erection, prayed to Jesus for forgiveness, and cut my throat with my Boy Scout penknife before I reached the ground. All my nerves are knotted up with love, and I don't know who I'm in love with. Maybe it's because my mother is so overheated today, maybe that's infectious . . .

(DRIVER returns to the cab. GHOST upside down from trapdoor in upper deck. DRIVER hangs his head.)

No I haven't done Claud yet, Dad. It sort of slipped my mind. Been one of those days. One of those days when you say to yourself, 'There's something I forgot to do, what was it? I've adjusted my rear-view mirrors, I've filled up the tank, I've dusted the conductress — but there was something, something, what was it? I know. I forgot to murder my uncle.'

(GHOST turns away in disgust, then turns back and shakes both fists.)

See what I can do. But if I do it, will you stop this haunting lark?

(GHOST nods emphatically.)

You won't be doomed to lurk around the route any more?

(GHOST shakes head.)

What'll you do then?

(GHOST grins, pulls himself into upper deck. Gold light on upper deck. GHOST picks up harp and begins to strum.)

You'll go to heaven? Very pleased to hear it. But what about me? Where'll I go?

(Red light on Cab. DRIVER writhes amid flames, picks up trident and mimes being tormented by devils. CONDUCTRESS stirs, opens one eye. GHOST exits.)

CONDUCTRESS: Stop wriggling, Owen. Stop wriggling and get married.

(The POLKA-DOT NUN climbs onto lower deck. She has an A-Z London street guide and some crayons. Her black habit is decorated with white polka dots. She starts to colour the book. CONDUCTRESS snoozes on. INSPECTOR marches on.)

INSPECTOR (to DRIVER): I have been empowered to say that the distur-bances on this vehicle are intolerable to the authorities. I have top-level orders that from tomorrow morning this bus will be bugged. Now — get moving, you swinehound. And put your lights on —

(Headlights on.)

— Not those —

(Sidelights on.)

— right. Blinding the poor buggers.

(INSPECTOR bending over CONDUCTRESS for a Prince Charming kiss when at the last moment he observes NUN watching with a smile.)

Now sister, you do your job and I'll do mine, right?

NUN: Quite right, Inspector, but you see I am doing my job. I am illuminating the 120 pages of maps in the A to Z London Street Directory. I'm colouring each patch of grass green, each row of houses red, each stretch of water blue and each road a dark purple tarmac colour. And I am giving each street and square a new name of religious significance and inscribing its new name in gold ink with my mapping pen.

INSPECTOR: What's in it for you?

NUN: It's a penance for my manifold sins.

INSPECTOR: Let me inspect it.

NUN: No.

INSPECTOR: Why not?

NUN: It's a work of art.

INSPECTOR: So you won't show it to anyone?

NUN: No, it's too beautiful for the eyes of sinners. And we're all sinners, aren't we? If I met St Francis of Assisi I might let him have a quick glance through this beautiful book. And then I'd take it back. It is my present for God and nobody else. You're not God, are you?

INSPECTOR: You want me to be frank?

(NUN nods.)

I'm not actually God.

NUN: Well you can piss off then. Just a moment. Inspector, it's a bizarre thing but you remind me of someone, name's on the tip of my tongue, don't tell me —

INSPECTOR: Not another? You don't mean —

(Going into Frankie Howard routine.)

To be. Aah. Yerss. To be or not to be — no, listen. No, the thing is this. To be. To be or not to be, that is the question. Yerss. The quest-i-on. Yerss. No, listen. Whether 'tis nobler in the mind — the mind missus, the mind. No, you wouldn't would you? Poor soul, no, don't mock the afflicted. No, you see. No, listen. No, the thing is this, whether 'tis nobler in the mind to suffer the slings and arrows of *outrageous* fortune — well, is it? Is it?

(As INSPECTOR.)

Yes, we're related on the side.

NUN: Ah! Yes – Billy Graham!

INSPECTOR: But you told me to piss off. What sort of nun are you?

NUN: I'm a temporary nun.

INSPECTOR: Never heard of such a thing.

NUN (walking to platform): I'm on a limited lease to God. Got to do a three-year stretch of poverty, chastity and obedience.

INSPECTOR: What do you do when your time's up?

NUN: I'm going to the South Seas to join my boyfriend.

CONDUCTRESS: What's he like then?

(NUN rings bell and off bus to dance and sing.)

> In a broken-down hut
> Lives the polka-dot coconut man
> He's a poker faced nut
> Of a hocus-pocus joker called Dan.
> Cut a lot of holes in your swimsuit
> If you want to get a polka-dot tan
> Says my hottentot, rotten-lot
> Polka-dot coconut man.
>
> Economically he's a disaster
> Philosophically he's nothing at all
> Clams in the ocean move faster
> All that he has is a ball.
>
> I'm a poker, red-hot,
> For that polka-dot coconut man.
> And I'll give all I've got
> To fan him with my polka-dot fan.
> Smoking bananas by moonlight
> With my bloke having polka-dot fun
> I'll be the broken-up woken-up
> Polka-dot coconut nun.

CONDUCTRESS: Victoria Street! Abbey box office! Book here for all entertainments and travel.

NUN (walking into bus slowly, fingering its seats and sides): I'd like to launch a formal complaint, Inspector, about the interior of this bus. It seems to me that the surface of the seats is dank and moist like the fur of bad animals. The hand-rails are alive with cold sweat. The ceiling is coated with soft yellow substance like the tongue of a smoker. And over every part of the fixtures and fittings is smeared a thin layer of slime.

INSPECTOR: Well I can't –

(Feeling the fixtures.)

I don't *think* there's any truth.

NUN: You don't feel the damp and the slime Inspector? Is it perhaps that your own fingers are already covered with a similar slime?

INSPECTOR (as NUN leaves): Perhaps you're right, you could be, yes that seems . . . .

(Slightly hypnotized.)

Myfanwy! Get this bus taken to the de-sliming depot at Hounslow tonight.

CONDUCTRESS: She's playing on your guilt feelings, Claud.

INSPECTOR: Guilt! I don't feel guilty.

DRIVER: Then you don't feel nothing.

(To the NUN.)

There's nothing sordid about this bus. You've got dirty eyes, that's why you see it dirty. But it's a clean machine and that's the truth. Truth? You wouldn't dare to face the truth.

INSPECTOR (going to him): All right, son —

DRIVER: Driver Stubber to you.

INSPECTOR: All right, Driver Stubber, you asked for it. What is truth?

DRIVER: Marie Lloyd.

INSPECTOR: How can the truth be Marie Lloyd?

DRIVER: Because the greatest concentration of human heat that this metropolis has ever known was embodied in the small but robust figure of Marie Lloyd.

CONDUCTRESS: Sing him the song, Owen.

DRIVER (sings to the tune of 'Calon Lan'):
Marie Lloyd was warm as kettles
And as frank as celluloid.
And her words could sting like nettles
Or caress like Marie Lloyd.

Marie Lloyd, come back and warm us.
Marie Lloyd, return to us,
For your heart was as enormous
As a double-decker bus.

Like a farted interruption
Of a talk by Sigmund Freud,
Like Mount Etna in eruption
Is the heart of Marie Lloyd.

DRIVER and CONDUCTRESS:
Marie Lloyd, come back and warm us.
Marie Lloyd, return to us,
For your heart is as enormous

As a double-decker bus

DRIVER:
She had eyes like Dylan Thomas
And the wit of Nye Bevan.
Marie Lloyd was taken from us —
Send her back to succour man.

DRIVER and CONDUCTRESS:
Marie Lloyd, come back and warm us.
Marie Lloyd, return to us.
For your heart is as enormous
As a double-decker bus.

(INSPECTOR, disgusted, puts his arm round CONDUCTRESS to escort her back on to the bus.)

DRIVER: I can't run him over with the bus while he's on board the bus. But for the first time I really want him to be dead. He grabbed her and took her away. Just now, I mean. You see, I love singing that song. With my mother. And we sang it. And then he grabbed her and took her away.

INSPECTOR: I'm getting worried about your son, Myfanwy, don't you think we should get him transferred to some quiet little country route —

CONDUCTRESS: Oh, he's terrible, but I'd miss him terribly . . .

(BISCUITS, concealed in MAHALIA's sack, appears on platform.)

INSPECTOR: Ah, you're the lady with the skin trouble, aren't you? Miss Revolting, 1973? Well, I've dealt with you once and I can deal with you twice.

(Assumes boxer's pose.)

Come to daddy.

(Large boxing glove appears from sack, thumps INSPECTOR on chin for a knock-out. BISCUITS takes off his sack.)

BISCUITS: I found his behaviour towards that poor girl on the outward trip excessively caddish. So I purloined her costume, swiftly perused a manual about the noble art and returned to give him what I believe is vulgarly known as a right good thumping.

(Exits. DRIVER comes round to platform. He and CONDUCTRESS stare down at the INSPECTOR.)

DRIVER: Why don't I get any?

CONDUCTRESS: The uniform plays some part in it, I think.

DRIVER: No, why don't I ever get any revenge? Everyone else is getting it. Everywhere I look, men getting their revenge on women, women getting their revenge on men, kids getting their revenge on parents.

CONDUCTRESS: Help me get your uncle on to one of the rear lateral seating units.

DRIVER: My uncle, mother? I think you mean your husband. Leave him to me.

(Furiously.)

Don't touch him.

(CONDUCTRESS shrugs, turns away. DRIVER hauls INSPECTOR into luggage compartment. Sotto voce to INSPECTOR.)

Before this bus is garaged tonight, I shall have chopped you so small that I can deposit you in the used ticket bin.

(DRIVER goes back to wheel. Starts up. CONDUCTRESS rings twice. Bus stops.)

CONDUCTRESS: Owen's in such a state. Pills might help, but I don't believe in pills. What he needs is a nice girl. We get a lot of girls who look nice on this bus. But they're often nasty girls in disguise. Whitehall. Any more for the Cenotaph?

(SOLDIER appears, face dead white, bloodstained bandage round his head, no rifle. He staggers to the platform.)

SOLDIER: Take me home.

CONDUCTRESS: Didn't you ride with us this morning?

SOLDIER: Can't remember. Take me home.

CONDUCTRESS: Where's home?

SOLDIER: Can't remember. Take me home.

DRIVER: You been in Ireland?

SOLDIER (jerking at the word Ireland): Yes. Can't remember. Yes. Take me home.

DRIVER: What can you remember?

SOLDIER: What day is it today? Take me home.

CONDUCTRESS: Friday.

SOLDIER: Take me home. I remember Friday.

(Sings.)
    I was working for a farmer
    But I answered him back.
    Got my wages on the Friday,
    Plus the sack.
    When I talked about the union,
    The farmer said to me:

FARMER (appearing on the platform, sings):
    Don't you know what day
    This happens to be?

    It's fuck off Friday,

    That's the day I love.
    When all of the losers
    Get the shove.
    I call it my day,
    I can't wait till when
    Fuck off Friday
    Rolls round again.

SOLDIER (sings):
    Used to do a bit of dancing,
    Rock 'n' roll.
    My fiancee chucked me
    'Cos I was on the dole
    Went down for a handout
    To the N.A.B.
    But the bird behind the counter
    Said:

CLERK (appearing in downstairs window of bus, sings):
    Can't you see?

    It's fuck off Friday
    That's the day I love.
    When all of the losers
    Get the shove.
    I call it my day,
    I can't wait till when
    Fuck off Friday
    Rolls round again.

SOLDIER (sings):
    So I joined the Army
    For the regular pay.
    At least the British Army
    Never turns you away.
    I was walking through Derry,
    Got a shot in the head.
    And as I lay dying
    An angel said:

ANGEL (sings):
    It's fuck off Friday,
    That's the day I love.
    When all of the losers
    Get the shove.
    I call it my day,
    I can't wait till when
    Fuck off Friday
    Rolls round again.

SOLDIER (sings):
>Well the British Army
>Bought my coffin and wreath
>And my mother got a cable
>From Edward Heath.
>But when she read his
>Condolence note,
>She sent him back a letter —
>Here's what she wrote:

SOLDIER'S MOTHER (sings):
>It's fuck off Friday
>That's the day I love.
>When all the Tories
>Get the shove,
>I call it my day,
>I can't wait till when
>Fuck off Friday
>Comes to number ten.

ALL (abandoning their 'song characters', sing):
>Saturday . . . Sunday . . . Monday . . .
>Tuesday . . . Wednesday . . . Thursday . . .
>Fuck off Friday
>That's the day I love.
>When all of the bosses
>Get the shove.
>I call it my day,
>I can't wait till when
>Fuck off Friday
>Comes to number ten.

INSPECTOR (coming round): No dead men allowed on this bus.

SOLDIER: Take me home.

DRIVER: Let's take him home.

INSPECTOR: Technically, this soldier is a corpse. There are regulations against corpses. There are penalties.

CONDUCTRESS: We don't know where to drop him.

DRIVER: All right, if you want him off the bus — you dump him. Take him over the street, that's where he belongs.

INSPECTOR (takes SOLDIER out): Come along squire, let's be having you.

SOLDIER: Take me home.

>(INSPECTOR and SOLDIER exit.)

DRIVER: He's putting him in the right place. Right where all the corpses should be dumped.

CONDUCTRESS: Isn't that where the Prime Minister lives?

(DRIVER smiles and nods, Goes back to cab. LORD BASIE, a gourmet, and LORD ELLINGTON, with a golf bag, get on the bus. Bus starts.)

BASIE: Funny to be travelling on a bus, what? My mother always told me that to be seen on a bus after the age of thirty meant that one had been a failure in life, eh?

ELLINGTON: Well if you hadn't written off your Jag swerving to avoid that fatuous cyclist we'd be home and dry by now. Jesus! I had a fabulous round this morning. Topped my first four tee-shots and three-pulled on the seventh green.

BASIE: You know what I could do with? Dinner at Bumbles. Prawn almond and egg mayonnaise, coquille St Jacques with a rosemary-flavoured sauce, honeyed spare ribs with onions and beans and some enchiladas.

ELLINGTON: But then I took a long, power-packed swing, high into the wind and all of 280 yards down the fairway. Wish you could have seen my caddy's face.

(CONDUCTRESS is waiting for their fares. They ignore her.)

BASIE: Or perhaps a really good tuck-in at the Mirabelle. Underdone roast partridge, langoustines au whisky or dressed drab. Or perhaps miniature quiches and veal sweetbreads at the Snooty Fox.

ELLINGTON: You'll never believe it, but at the short eighth I hit the stick with my chip from 30 yards and the pill plonked in.

(To CONDUCTRESS.)

What is it, darling?

CONDUCTRESS: This machine is a bus. You pay. You pay money.

BASIE: How quaint.

(Produces credit card.)

Two bloodytories to number 33 Grosvenor Square, savvy? Or perhaps a sea-bass fillet with crumbly stuffing at the Capital Hotel?

ELLINGTON: Was playing a fourball for a fiver a corner. I skewed into the rough at the tenth, but then I wedged it on to the green and holed out for a birdie five.

CONDUCTRESS: Well you can hole out of here. It's not a taxi. Trafalgar Square! Bloody South Africa House!

(Rings bell, bus stops.)

BASIE: No need to take that tone with us.

ELLINGTON: No call for that kind of impudence.

BASIE: Absolutely not. We don't pay super-tax in order to be insulted by raddled old bags with red hands and inflatable tits.

ELLINGTON: No, we don't take lip from a tramp's left-overs.

CONDUCTRESS: Shitholes and bollock-chops – get off my fucking bus!

BASIE (leaving): Actually, I know where we could get a halibut marinated in lime juice and garnished with avocado. Quails would be nice . . .

ELLINGTON: My 3-iron has grooves cut in the sole so that the clubhead can be kept lower to the ground while taking a divot after slicing the ball . . .

(BASIE and ELLINGTON exit. CONDUCTRESS sits and puts her head in her hands.)

CONDUCTRESS (very upset): What if I am a rotten old bag? They didn't have to say so. The worst thing in the world is the way some people treat other people.

(DRIVER comes back to her.)

The worst thing in the world is the way some people treat other people. The worst thing in the world –

DRIVER: What's up Mum? Do you want to stop for a drink.

CONDUCTRESS: Why can't they be a bit gentle?

DRIVER: Gentle? What do you know about being gentle? You're tough as a jeep.

CONDUCTRESS: You drive over the sort of tracks I've driven over, you better be a bloody Sherman tank. But I am a gentle person. I've been gentle several times. As a baby I was well-known in Dollgellau for my lack of viciousness. When I was eight, and Dai Roberts was five, he tripped over his laces in the school playground and got a kneefull of gravel. So I sucked out the little stones and bound up his wound with my hankie. And the preacher was talking to Miss Griffiths and he turned around and saw me abandaging and: 'Who's that gentle little girl?' He said, 'Who's that gentle little girl?' Course he hadn't see me sucking the knee.

DRIVER: If he had he might have misconstrued your solicitude as salacity.

CONDUCTRESS: And he might have been right. Then Dai Roberts lost my hankie, so I had to bash him till he gave me his Saturday sixpence to buy another. Well, I bashed him as gently as I could. If I hadn't bashed him my mam would have bashed me for losing the hankie.

DRIVER: You weren't very gentle with me.

(To audience.)

Had the kick of a Llanelli fullback.

CONDUCTRESS: Only kicked you. Never laid a fist on you. I was trying to be gentle.

DRIVER: You're forgetting. That night you walked over to the little knight in armour from the co-op standing in the fireplace. And you opened his vizor and you took out the hearthbrush and then you let me have it across the pyjamas. Winceyette.

CONDUCTRESS: That was later. That was in England.

DRIVER: That was me. That was you.

CONDUCTRESS: I'd had a lot of your Dad by then. I'd had a lot of bronchitis. I'd had a lot of unemployment. I'd had a lot of moving house, moving country. Moving out of Wales into bloody England for a bloody job. My gentleness was all down the drain.

DRIVER: I'm sorry. You are gentle really. In real life.

CONDUCTRESS: But this isn't real life is it — seven hours a day being bumped around on a bus? Doesn't leave you feeling very gentle.

DRIVER: Is my uncle Claud gentle?

CONDUCTRESS: Yes. Oh no, he's not gentle at all.

DRIVER: All right. Cry. Sleep. London Transport schedules can get stuffed.

(CONDUCTRESS kips down on seat, DRIVER on to the forestage.)

I've got to do it. I've got to run Claud over. I suppose I can do it. I've only run over one bloke before, and that was an accident, on my part anyway. He was an old man and he threw himself under my radiator — his skull went pop. I couldn't hear it pop, but I could feel the pop through my offside front tyre. I was driving a Routemaster 47 at the time, a comparatively sensitive vehicle. Anyway I backed up, into neutral, pulled on the handbrake and climbed down to scrape him off. A cop had already gone through his pockets and the cop said to me: 'You know who you flattened, Jim?' 'No,' I said. 'Well,' he said, 'that bloke was 90 years old and he was retired. Guess what his job was?' 'Can't,' I said. 'Well he was the chap whose job it was to hold a bowl for the public hangman in case he wanted to vomit.' 'That's nice,' I said, 'holding a bowl for that bugger.' Then I took a step back, slipped in the blood and landed with my face splat in the old bloke's brains. Well I wiped it off with my hanky. But some of the juice from the brain of the man who used to hold the vomit bowl for the hangman splashed into my mouth. And do you know what his brains tasted like? The *Daily* Bloody *Telegraph*.

(CHARLIE WEBB, a black revolutionary, jeans, rough old jacket, hurries on.)

CHARLIE: Hide me. They're after me.

CONDUCTRESS: What's up?

DRIVER: They're after him.

CONDUCTRESS: Hide him — go on, up the stairs.

(CONDUCTRESS pushes CHARLIE in front of her up the stairs. Two COPS come on.)

FIRST COP (to DRIVER): Seen any coons?

DRIVER: Not me.

SECOND COP: Well watch out for a coon.

(COPS go out.)

DRIVER: Never seen anyone I'd call a coon. OK, they've gone.

(CHARLIE follows CONDUCTRESS down the stairs. CHARLIE draws pistol on DRIVER and CONDUCTRESS.)

CHARLIE: Into the cab. Both of you.

DRIVER: Look we've got nothing against you.

CHARLIE: Then get into the cab.

(DRIVER, CONDUCTRESS and CHARLIE climb into the cab.)

Now get me out of London.

CONDUCTRESS: It's a number 24, it's never been further than Hampstead Heath.

CHARLIE: Drive.

(DRIVER revs up and begins to drive faster than usual.)

CONDUCTRESS: Why are they chasing you?

CHARLIE: They think I killed a politician.

DRIVER: Did you?

CHARLIE: I shot at him. Hope he's dead.

DRIVER: Look mate, you can't go round shooting people in Britain.

CHARLIE: You wouldn't shoot Hitler, then? Not in England?

DRIVER: Hitler in England? I'd certainly feel like shooting him. Somebody probably would.

CHARLIE: The bloke I shot at was trying to be an English Hitler. I think he would've made it.

CONDUCTRESS: There'll be a backlash.

CHARLIE: There's a backlash already. Backlash. My great-grandparents were slaves. They knew about back lashes.

DRIVER: You weren't ever a slave, were you?

CHARLIE: No. But I didn't do badly for a free man.

DRIVER: You're all right. We're on your side really.

CHARLIE: Then what are you doing?

DRIVER: I know what I've got to do.

CHARLIE: Why haven't you done it?

DRIVER: I'm scared of prisons. Concrete. Bars. The screws. Nobody to hug you. I've had mates been in the nick. They come out looking like ghosts all lost, don't know what's real and what's not. And then they drift back in again, into the nick where they know what's real. Concrete.

Bars. And the screws. So I've put it off. But next time I'm going to do it.

CHARLIE: When I see what you do, I'll see if we're on the same side. But I'm not taking chances. You're workers but a lot of workers still think that the enemies of the poor are the blacks, the reds, the yellows and the browns. The enemies of the poor are the rich. I've overheard rich men talking about the poor. And if the poor could hear just one of those conversations, the Revolution would start now.

CONDUCTRESS: But when's this Revolution really going to come?

CHARLIE: When you least expect it.

(Riot COPS with guns burst on to the stage.)

DRIVER: Cops. They've put up a roadblock.

CHARLIE: Hit the brakes.

(Sings.)
    The good go to heaven and the bad to hell,
    But it doesn't always work out so neat.
    The hero's found hanging in his prison cell
    The villain dies of blondes in a penthouse suite.

    Now I know there's a product called freedom
    You can buy it in most of the shops.
    And I know that peace is science fiction
    But I also know the Revolution never stops.

    Everyone pays in the end they say,
    But I know one thing for sure:
    That the rich haven't even begun to pay
    For all they've done to the poor.

    Now I know there's a lady called Justice,
    'Cos I saw her boozing with the cops
    And I know that the blind are killing the blind,
    But I also know the revolution never stops
    Yes I also know the Revolution never stops.

FIRST COP: Stop him!

(CHARLIE makes a feint of surrendering, then jumps off edge of the stage and down the aisle as DRIVER on headlights, blinding COPS. CHARLIE escapes through door of theatre. FIRST COP approaches.)

Now that's a very serious offence —

(CONDUCTRESS flings herself into DRIVER's arms.)

FATHER XMAS (appearing on upper deck): Ho, ho, ho. Hold everything.

(COP freeze again. Snow begins to fall.)

Ho, ho, ho, my jolly young friends! I've come to grant your wishes with my magic powers.

DRIVER: But it's not Christmas, it's not nearly Christmas.

FATHER XMAS: Oh ye of little faith – haven't you heard the news?

> (Sings while COPS dance.)
>> Capitalism is Christmas every day
>> Capitalism is Christmas in every way
>> We all share the profits
>> Nobody makes a loss
>> It's the happy marriage
>> Of the worker and his boss
>> Merrily merrily we are here to say
>> That Capitalism is Christmas every day.

> (DRIVER and CONDUCTRESS are staring at each other. They are realizing that they love each other.)

> Right I've promised to grant your wishes. What would you respected guardians of the law and order like best in the world?

COPS (in chorus): We don't want to be bloody cops any more.

FATHER XMAS: No sooner wished than granted. Ho, ho, ho! Ho, ho, ho!

> (Ad nauseam.)

> (FATHER XMAS waves hands. Explosion of lights. Blackout. Lights up on COPS out of uniform into everyday casual clothes, whatever they like. They are now themselves. Enter GHOST.)

> I don't see why a spectre shouldn't have a wish. What is it?

> (GHOST points to tongue.)

> Ah, God's gift of speech.

> (Makes magic passes.)

> Owen Stubber Senior, you are healed.

GHOST (after trying out tongue): So much to tell you, Myfanwy, don't know where to start –

CONDUCTRESS: Who said that?

FATHER XMAS: Apologies all round. I forgot that only myself and young Owen can see our phantom friend. But that's easily solved with new improved visibility dust.

> (Sprinkles dust over GHOST.)

CONDUCTRESS: Where've you been, Owen?

GHOST: All over the shop. First I went to heaven. Like a posh cocktail bar it is. They had a hi-fi playing The Sacred Side of Cliff Richard. I elbowed my way through this crowd of bishops and bagged a stool between Moses and Malcolm Muggeridge. Jesus was at the sink with a teacloth marked A Souvenir of Gethsemane, polishing up the Holy Grail. And then I saw the landlord, God. Big chap he was. Handlebar moustache, tweed suit,

R.A.F. tie. Evening, Stubber, he said to me, what's your poison? Pint of Newcastle Brown, I said, thin glass please, God. Sorry, old bean, he said, Heaven is a doubles bar. All right, I said, a large whisky Mac. So I took a sip. Nothing. Took a gulp. Nothing. Drained it. Nothing. Hey, I said, excuse me, your honour, this stuff's got about as much kick as flat Tizer. Well, God looked at me, and he said: some of the chappies up here have been boozing for five thousand years. Continuous. No closing time in Heaven. If we put alcohol in the Scotch the place would be full of holy drunks. Baptists wouldn't like it. So I slipped out. Sooner spend eternity haunting the buses. And getting my revenge on the bastard who —

FATHER XMAS: Come come, season of goodwill. What about you, Owen Stubber Junior? Make a wish.

DRIVER: Can't.

FATHER XMAS: Why not?

DRIVER: You see I need two wishes. One's no good without the other.

FATHER XMAS: Shall I give him two?

EX-COPS ETC: Yeah, go on, give him two.

DRIVER: But they're naughty wishes. Wicked Welsh wishes.

CONDUCTRESS: Please state your destination clearly.

DRIVER: Don't know how to.

FATHER XMAS: Try one wish at a time.

DRIVER (to Audience): Shall I? All right, I'll whisper.

(Big stage whisper to FATHER XMAS.)

Wish one. I want to kill my Uncle Claud.

FATHER XMAS: Well, here he comes.

(All freeze. INSPECTOR enters in sinister overcoat.)

INSPECTOR (aside): I overheard young Owen swear to kill me when he thought I'd been knocked out. And I'm afraid that he suspects the truth about my secret identity.

(Opening overcoat to show badge.)

So I dipped the pin of my Inspector's badge in poison. Where did I get the poison, do I hear you cry? I had it off a mountebank. Have you ever had it off a mountebank?

(Significant pause. Suddenly ALL unfreeze.)

DRIVER: Turn and face your Nemesis, you dirty old trolley.

(INSPECTOR and DRIVER unpin their badges and face each other like fencers. OTHERS crowd round.)

I know your real name.

(INSPECTOR and DRIVER begin to fence, urged on by the OTHERS.

INSPECTOR's pin forced from his hand to the ground, but he kicks DRIVER to the floor, where DRIVER loses his pin. Silently, they mutually agree to pause and remove their coats. CONDUCTRESS picks up the pins and sniffs them.)

CONDUCTRESS: Poison! Oh, Claud! I'll swap the pins.

(CONDUCTRESS swaps pins from hand to hand and gives them back to INSPECTOR and DRIVER. Fight begins again, DRIVER, with a sudden yell, chases INSPECTOR up stairs of bus, where they fight over the seats of the upper deck, until DRIVER, missing the INSPECTOR, is stabbed in the arse by his opponent.)

DRIVER: Aaraagh!

(Undramatically.)

Jesus Christ, that hurt.

(INSPECTOR sniffs his pin, suddenly realizes.)

INSPECTOR: She swapped the pins!

(INSPECTOR hurtles down the stairs. DRIVER leaps from upper deck to stage and confronts him at the platform, chasing him down the lower saloon. As they fence desperately, GHOST switches on the bus's flashing indicator lights, thus distracting INSPECTOR's attention. DRIVER stabs INSPECTOR in the chest. INSPECTOR collapses along the keyboard of the piano, then staggers forward.)

Dying speech. Listen to my last words. That is an order. I am not Claud. I am not a bus Inspector. I spit on Claud. I spit on buses. I spit on Picasso. I was a painter, once. I drew a poster for Teddy's Perspiration Powder in Vienna. Many buses run into Russia but there are no buses coming back. I was a final solution. Some got away. Goebbels got a job on BBC2. I buried my parachute near Betws-y-Coed. Where are my monkey-gland pills? They keep me going. Don't hit me. Hit me. Hit me with a bus and bury me under the number 89 route from Munich to Berlin. This is the last territorial claim that I shall make in Europe. Give me paper. I was a painter once.

(CONDUCTRESS gives him paper.)

Oh blitz me, Eva! A conspiracy of international bus-drivers squashed my paintings under their sickening wheels.

(INSPECTOR is painting on the paper with his fingers dipped in his own blood.)

She was as beautiful as bombers. Keep your pity, I want your terror. I wear a black moustache to give you nightmares. And your nightmares will all come true. Achtung! A portrait of my own true love.

(Shows his painting – a swastika in blood.)

Goering, there's a Spitfire in my soup. I am a sympathetic character. What's six million? There is no such place as Auschwitz. I sympathize with myself. Churchill would love me if he knew me. Somebody tell me quickly, my staff have taken cyanide, so somebody tell me – is it true that the Beatles are Jewish? Hitler rules, OK?

(Dies.)

DRIVER (recites to music):
There's one more Nazi
Ready for the grave.
He'll behave in the grave.
Power to the grave.

(DRIVER breaking into song and Cliff imitation to 'Power to All Our Friends.')

Bollocks to all our foes
Whether Hitlers or Uncle Joes.
To the boss and the bourgeoisie
Baby, bollocks from you and me.

(DRIVER freezes in showy pose. OTHERS hold up placards with low numbers on.)

FATHER XMAS: Better luck next year. But you've granted the old horror, so that's your first wish granted. What's your second?

DRIVER: I want to marry my mother.

CONDUCTRESS (embracing him): Oh that's a lovely wish. But can we do it?

FATHER XMAS: I don't see why not, given the recent leap forward in contraceptive techniques. Strikes me as an excellent idea. You're sure it's not just infatuation, or a dream that will fade and fall apart?

DRIVER and CONDUCTRESS: Oh no, it's love.

CONDUCTRESS (to GHOST): You do understand if I marry Owen, don't you Owen?

GHOST: Well I'n not much use for it now, am I? You can't stop living your own life, Myfanwy. I suppose I'll just have to go on dying my own death. A little tipple would help though.

(FATHER XMAS gives him a huge whisky bottle.)

Bless you, my children.

FATHER XMAS: In that case, mother and son, I pronounce you man and wife.

(EX-COPS cheer. DRIVER and CONDUCTRESS embrace.)

FATHER XMAS (sings music-hall style):
M – A – double R – Y
Your m–o–t–h–e–r.
Don't be shy, my little laddie,
She was good enough for daddy!
Boom! Boom! Back to the womb!

    Where'd you get that mum from?
    Marry your mother today
    And go back where you come from!

(Enter VIKING. ALL dance on spot and music continues.)

VIKING (reading from his book): A buzz-driver from Sor Trandelag who suffered from headaches went to see a psychiatrist. After the consultation the psychiatrist called in the buzz-driver's mother. He looked at her solemnly, 'I'm afraid,' he informed her, 'that your son is suffering from an Oedipus complex.' 'Oedipus-Yoedipus!' She exclaimed, 'What do I care so long as he can still drive a buzz!'

(ALL, except INSPECTOR's corpse, sing and dance.)

ALL:
    M — A — double R — Y
    Your M-O-T-H-E-R,
    Don't be shy, my little laddie,
    She was good enough for Daddy!
    Boom! Boom! back to the womb!
    Where'd you'd get that mum from?
    Marry your mother today
    And go back where you come from!

CONDUCTRESS: Do I get a wish too?

FATHER XMAS: Of course.

CONDUCTRESS: I want the bus.

DRIVER: That's a good wish. But what'll you do with it?

CONDUCTRESS: Drive around with it, give people free lifts. Liberate the bus and take it back to Wales. I must be able to take it to Wales.

(Sings unaccompanied.)
    Nid wy'n gofyn bywyd moethus,
    Aury byd na berlau man;
    Gofyn wyf am galon hapus,
    Calon onest, calon lan.

    Calon lan yn llawn daioni,
    Tecach yw na'r lili dlos:
    Does ond calon lan all ganu —
    Canu'r dydd a chanu'r nos.

FIRST EX-COP: Can I come too? I'm Welsh.

SECOND EX-COP: What about me? I'm Welsher than he is.

OTHER EX-COPS: So are we. We're all Welsh.

(CONDUCTRESS waves them aboard.)

VIKING: Can I be nationalized?

CONDUCTRESS: I'll do it myself on the journey.

GHOST: I may be a phantom. But I'm a Welsh phantom.

DRIVER: Where to?

CONDUCTRESS: To Wales.

(ALL on bus produce Welsh flags — one big one.)

FATHER XMAS: Just before you go, there's something I don't understand. That bus of yours is full of crazy people.

DRIVER: That's right. Daft as doughnuts.

FATHER XMAS: And now they've all suddenly turned into Welsh Nationalists? What's that in aid of?

DRIVER: Look, we've been trundling round and round route 24 for centuries. Round and round, that's a treadmill. But now we're going to run free, we're going to zig-zag all over Wales. Having fun, making trouble. And we're going to stick a giant sun-ray lamp on the top of the bus suntan all the Taffy population till they're as black as bibles.

(Enter actor who played CHARLIE.)

EX-CHARLIE: Hallelujah!

EX-COPS: Right on!

(EX-CHARLIE on bus.)

FATHER XMAS: That's not very logical.

DRIVER: Logic would only get us as far as Slough. We're going to Wales.

FATHER XMAS: But why Wales?

DRIVER (impatiently): Because we like bloody Wales.

(Roller changes to Welsh dragon and the word CYMRU.)

ALL (sing):
    Pe dymunwn olud bydol,
    Aidain fuan ganddo sydd;
    Golud calon lan, rinweddol
    Yn dwyn bythol elw fydd.

    Calon lan yn llawn daioni —
    Tecach yw na'r lili dlos;
    Does ond calon lan all ganu —
    Canu'r dydd a chanu'r nos.

    Hwyr a bore fy nymuniad
    Gwyd i'r nef ar adain can
    Ar dduw, er mwyn fy ngheidwade,
    Roddi imi calon lan.

    Calon lan yn llawn daioni
    Tecach yw na'r lili dlos;
    Does ond calon lan all ganu —
    Canu'r dydd a chanu'r nos.

(VIKING lowers a song-sheet from upper deck.)

Marie Lloyd was warm as kettles
And as frank as celluloid.
And her words could sting like nettles
Or caress like Marie Lloyd.

Marie Lloyd, come back and warm us.
Marie Lloyd, return to us,
For your heart is as enormous
As a double-decker bus.

**The end**

The photograph overleaf shows the set designed
        by Peter Ling for the London production. ▶

Photo: Nobby Clarke

# OVERTURE

*Brisk and Sloppy*

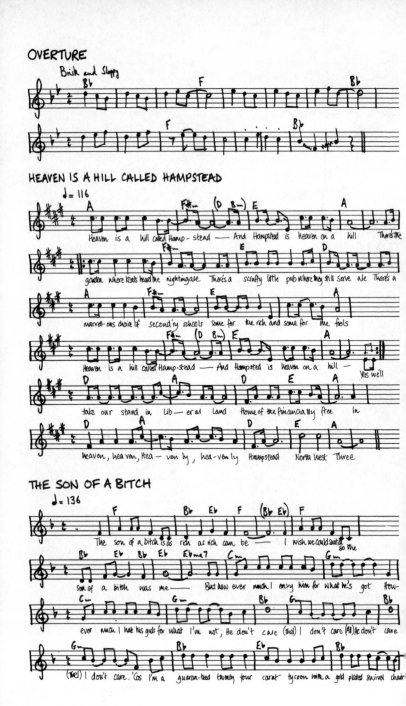

# HEAVEN IS A HILL CALLED HAMPSTEAD

♩ = 116

Heaven is a hill called Hamp-stead —— And Hampstead is heaven on a hill There's the garden where Keats heard the nightingale There's a scruffy little pub where they still serve ale There's a marvell-ous choice of second'ry schools some for the rich and some for the fools Heaven is a hill called Hamp-stead —— And Hampstead is heaven on a hill —— Yes we'll take our stand in lib—er-al Land Home of the financially free In heaven, hea-ven, Hea—ven-ly, hea-ven-ly Hampstead North West Three

# THE SON OF A BITCH

♩ = 136

The son of a bitch is as rich as rich can be —— I wish we could switch so the son of a bitch was me —— But how ever much I envy him for what he's got How-ever much I hate his guts for what I'm not, He don't care (Tho') I don't care (All) He don't care (Tho') I don't care. 'Cos I'm a guaran-teed twenty four carat tycoon with a gold plated swivel chair

# ROUTE 24

## WASH YOUR HANDS

## HERE I COMES

## A SPELL TO MAKE A BAD TIME PASS

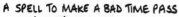

OH THAT TUB!

Must have smoke beneath from your agar   Oh my tub   My grand ol' wooden tub
I'll make up for all they're done to you   Just you
wait   I won't be late   I'm going to fix you up like new, 'cause
I've got paint   and I've got   glue   Oh that tub   You
grand ol' wooden   tub. (Spoken ad lib) I'm coming back. We'll always be together. Oh you tub
Tub, Tub, Tub, Tuuuuuuub!

## BALL GAME SONG (Unaccompanied)

One, one, bounce the ball Once for the sandal maker — Two, two, bounce the ball twice for the
fisherman on the river Three, three, bounce the ball Three times for your gol-den lover.

## THE WORST THING IN THE WORLD

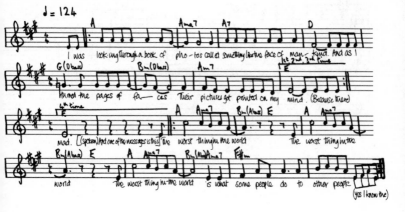

♩ = 124

I was looking through a book of pho-tos called something like the face of man-kind And as I
turned the pages of fa — ces Their pictures got printed on my mind. (Because there's)
mad. (Spoken) And one of the messages is this. The worst thing in the world   the worst thing in the
world   The worst thing in the world   is what some people do to other people. (Yes I know the)

# THE LITTLE RED SCHOOLGIRL

# EVERY HOME SHOULD HAVE ONE

Smile if you had sex last night Hey you know a-my place I can crash? Would-be leaders shoot on sight but first I've got to get my stash. We'll turn the low-er East Side in-to a woodland glade — You know a man must make his move be-fore his name is made And ev'ry home should have one Ev'ry home should h-have one —

First 4 lines of Verse 5 are sung an 8ve below written

# ROYAL PARADE MUSIC

Breakneck Tempo

1st time    2nd (or last) time

# THE POLKA-DOT COCONUT MAN

In a broken down hut lives the polka dot co-co-nut man — He's a poker faced nut of a hocus pocus joker called Dan Cut a lot of holes in your swim-suit If you want get a polka dot tan Says my hotten-tot rotten lot polka dot co-conut m-man — Eco-nomically he's a dis-as-ter Philo-sophic'ly he's nothing at all

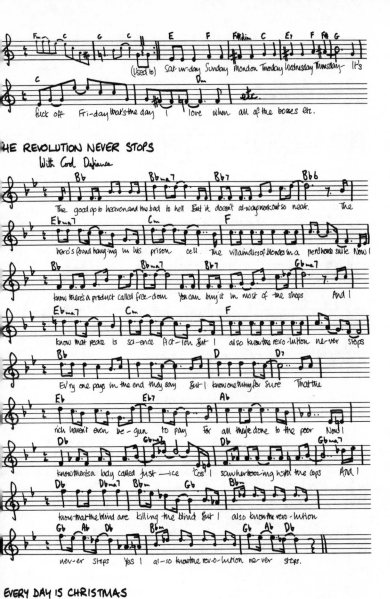

## METHUEN PLAYSCRIPTS

| | |
|---|---|
| Michael Abbensetts | SWEET TALK |
| Paul Ableman | TESTS |
| | BLUE COMEDY |
| Andrei Amalrik | EAST-WEST and IS UNCLE JACK A CONFORMIST? |
| Ed Berman/Justin Wintle | THE FUN ART BUS |
| Barry Bermange | NATHAN AND TABILETH AND OLDENBERG |
| John Bowen | THE CORSICAN BROTHERS |
| Howard Brenton | REVENGE |
| | CHRISTIE IN LOVE and OTHER PLAYS |
| | PLAYS FOR PUBLIC PLACES |
| | MAGNIFICENCE |
| Henry Chapman | YOU WON'T ALWAYS BE ON TOP |
| Peter Cheeseman (Ed) | THE KNOTTY |
| Caryl Churchill | OWNERS |
| David Cregan | THREE MEN FOR COLVERTON |
| | TRANSCENDING AND THE DANCERS |
| | THE HOUSES BY THE GREEN |
| | MINIATURES |
| | THE LAND OF PALMS AND OTHER PLAYS |
| Alan Cullen | THE STIRRINGS IN SHEFFIELD ON SATURDAY NIGHT |
| Rosalyn Drexler | THE INVESTIGATION and HOT BUTTERED ROLL |
| Simon Gray | THE IDIOT |
| Henry Livings | GOOD GRIEF! |
| | THE LITTLE MRS FOSTER SHOW |
| | HONOUR AND OFFER |
| | PONGO PLAYS 1-6 |
| | THIS JOCKEY DRIVES LATE NIGHTS |
| | THE FFINEST FFAMILY IN THE LAND |
| | EH? |
| John McGrath | EVENTS WHILE GUARDING THE BOFORS GUN |
| David Mercer | THE GOVERNOR'S LADY |
| Georges Michel | THE SUNDAY WALK |
| Rodney Milgate | A REFINED LOOK AT EXISTENCE |
| Guillaume Oyono-Mbia | THREE SUITORS: ONE HUSBAND and UNTIL FURTHER NOTICE |
| Alan Plater | CLOSE THE COALHOUSE DOOR |
| David Selbourne | THE PLAY OF WILLIAM COOPER AND EDMUND DEW-NEVETT |
| | THE TWO-BACKED BEAST |
| | DORABELLA |

| | |
|---|---|
| Wole Soyinka | CAMWOOD ON THE LEAVES |
| Johnny Speight | IF THERE WEREN'T ANY BLACKS YOU'D HAVE TO INVENT THEM |
| Martin Sperr | TALES FROM LANDSHUT |
| Boris Vian | THE KNACKER'S ABC |
| Lanford Wilson | HOME FREE! and THE MADNESS OF LADY BRIGHT |
| Harrison, Melfi, Howard | NEW SHORT PLAYS |
| Duffy, Harrison, Owens | NEW SHORT PLAYS: 2 |
| Barker, Grillo, Haworth, Simmons | NEW SHORT PLAYS: 3 |

*If you would like regular information
on new Methuen plays, please write to
The Marketing Department
Eyre Methuen Ltd
North Way
Andover
Hants*